Schweizer Grand Prix Design

Grand Prix suisse de design   Gran Premio svizzero di design

Swiss Grand Award for Design

2021

Vorwort

Seit 2007 zeichnet das Bundesamt für Kultur die Werke von namhaften Designerinnen und Designern aus, die im nationalen und internationalen Kontext die Qualität und Relevanz der Schweizer Designpraxis repräsentieren. Kurz: Die Schweizer Grands Prix Design sind ein Spiegel des besten Schweizer Designs.

Dieses Jahr feiern wir das 15-jährige Bestehen des Preises. Die Liste der ehemaligen Preisträgerinnen und Preisträger zeichnet ein Bild, das repräsentativ ist für die Vielfalt der Designproduktion in der Schweiz. Die zahlreichen Positionen haben Impulse in der Schweizer Kulturlandschaft gesetzt, inspirieren neue Generationen von Gestalterinnen und Gestaltern und prägen das gegenwärtige Designschaffen sowie die Schweizer Designgeschichte.

Die Eidgenössische Designkommission entschied sich auch in diesem Jahr für drei herausragende Persönlichkeiten, die die nationale und internationale Designkultur beeinflusst haben. Es sind dies die Grafikdesignerin Julia Born, der Fotograf und Art Director Peter Knapp sowie die Forscherin und Dozentin Sarah Owens. Wir freuen uns sehr, Ihnen in der vorliegenden Publikation das Werk dieser drei Ausnahmetalente vorzustellen.

Das Buch liefert Ihnen ein Stück lebendige Designtradition: Die beiden Gewinnerinnen und der Gewinner werden mit einordnenden Texten, einer ausführlichen Biografie und repräsentativen Werkabbildungen vorgestellt. Zudem erhalten wir in umfassenden Gesprächen einen interessanten Einblick in spezifische Projekte, in konzeptuelle und kollaborative Arbeitsprozesse, aber auch in Forschung und Lehre mit interdisziplinären Ansätzen sowie einem erweiterten Designbegriff. Alle Inhalte sind in enger Zusammenarbeit mit den Preisträgerinnen und dem Preisträger entstanden.

Wir freuen uns die Schweizer Grand Prix Design Buchreihe nun als Serie in einem neuen Kleid zu lancieren. Jedes Jahr öffnet sich mit der spannenden Zusammenstellung von drei Persönlichkeiten aus ganz unterschiedlichen Berufsfeldern eine frische, inspirierende Optik auf die schweizerische Designwelt.

An dieser Stelle möchte ich mich besonders bei Julia Born, Peter Knapp und Sarah Owens sowie der Eidgenössischen Designkommission bedanken, die massgeblich und mit viel Engagement zum Gelingen dieses Buches beigetragen haben. Weiter gilt mein herzlicher Dank allen weiteren Beteiligten – der Koordinatorin, den Gestaltern, Autoren, Übersetzern, der Fotografin sowie den Korrektoren.

Préface

Depuis 2007, l'Office fédéral de la culture distingue des designers renommés dont l'œuvre témoigne de la qualité et de l'importance du design suisse dans le contexte national et international. En somme, les Grands Prix suisses de design sont un reflet de la meilleure production de notre pays en la matière.

Nous célébrons cette année le 15ᵉ anniversaire de la création de ce prix. La liste de ses lauréates et lauréats nous donne une image très représentative de la diversité de la production du design en Suisse. Ces nombreux créateurs et créatrices ont donné des impulsions importantes au paysage culturel de notre pays, inspiré de nouvelles générations de designers et marqué de leur empreinte la création contemporaine et l'histoire du design suisse.

Cette année encore, la Commission fédérale du design a choisi trois personnalités éminentes qui ont apporté une importante contribution à la culture nationale et internationale du design : la designer graphique Julia Born, le photographe et directeur artistique Peter Knapp et la chercheuse et enseignante Sarah Owens. C'est avec un grand plaisir que nous vous présentons dans cette publication l'œuvre de ces trois talents d'exception.

Cet ouvrage vous offre un morceau de la tradition vivante du design : les deux lauréates et le lauréat sont présentés par des textes introductifs, une biographie détaillée ainsi que des illustrations représentatives de leurs œuvres. En outre, des entretiens approfondis donnent un aperçu intéressant de projets spécifiques, de processus de travail conceptuels et collaboratifs, mais aussi de la recherche et de l'enseignement privilégiant des approches interdisciplinaires et une conception élargie de la notion de design. Tous ces éléments ont été élaborés en étroite collaboration avec les trois personnalités lauréates.

Nous sommes heureux de lancer la série d'ouvrages sur le Grand Prix suisse de design qui se présente dans un nouvel habillage. Chaque année, la passionnante compilation de trois personnalités issues d'horizons professionnels très divers pose un regard neuf et inspirant sur le monde du design suisse.

J'aimerais ici remercier tout particulièrement Julia Born, Peter Knapp et Sarah Owens ainsi que les membres de la Commission fédérale du design, qui, par leur grand engagement, ont apporté une contribution décisive à la qualité du présent ouvrage. Je remercie également toutes les autres personnes qui ont participé à sa publication : coordinatrice, graphistes, auteurs, traducteurs, photographe et correcteurs.

Prefazione

Dal 2007 l'Ufficio federale della cultura premia le opere di designer di spicco che riflettono la qualità e l'importanza del design svizzero nel contesto nazionale e internazionale. Concretamente, i Gran Premi svizzeri di design esaltano il meglio del design svizzero.

Quest'anno festeggiamo il 15° anniversario. L'elenco dei vincitori e delle vincitrici delinea un quadro rappresentativo di quanto varia sia la produzione di design in Svizzera. Queste personalità stimolano il paesaggio culturale svizzero, ispirando nuove generazioni di designer e plasmando le attuali correnti e la storia del design del nostro Paese.

Anche quest'anno la Commissione federale del design ha selezionato tre esponenti che hanno lasciato un segno nella cultura del design nazionale e internazionale. Si tratta della designer grafica Julia Born, del fotografo e direttore artistico Peter Knapp e della ricercatrice e docente Sarah Owens. Siamo lieti di poter presentare con questa pubblicazione l'opera di tre talenti eccezionali.

Questo volume rappresenta un pezzo di tradizione vivente del design: alle due vincitrici e al vincitore dedica approfondimenti contestuali, una biografia dettagliata e alcune illustrazioni rappresentative delle loro opere. Colloqui di ampio respiro ci regalano uno scorcio su progetti specifici, processi concettuali e collaborativi, ma anche su un lavoro interdisciplinare di ricerca e insegnamento, basato su una concezione estesa del design. Tutti i contenuti sono il risultato di una collaborazione diretta con le due vincitrici e il vincitore.

Siamo lieti di poter presentare i libri del Gran Premio svizzero di design, lanciati quest'anno in una nuova veste che li raccoglie in un'unica serie. Ogni anno il connubio di tre personalità provenienti da settori completamente diversi tra loro apre nuove stimolanti prospettive nel mondo del design svizzero.

Con l'occasione desidero ringraziare Julia Born, Peter Knapp, Sarah Owens e i membri della Commissione federale del design per il contributo determinante e il grande impegno profuso in questa pubblicazione. I miei ringraziamenti si estendono anche a tutte le altre persone che vi hanno preso parte sotto vari aspetti: coordinamento, redazione, traduzione, fotografia e correzione delle bozze.

Foreword

Since 2007, the Federal Office of Culture has honoured the work of well-known designers who exemplify the quality and relevance of Swiss design practice both nationally and internationally. Simply put, the Swiss Grand Awards for Design reflect the best that Switzerland has to offer in the field.

This year we celebrate 15 years since the award was created. The roll call of former winners illustrates the diverse spectrum of design production in Switzerland. In their many and varied ways, they have infused the Swiss cultural landscape with fresh ideas and continue to inspire new generations of designers, influencing current design as well as Swiss design history.

In 2021, the Federal Design Commission has again selected three outstanding personalities who have shaped national and international design culture. They are the graphic designer Julia Born, photographer and art director Peter Knapp, and researcher and lecturer Sarah Owens. We are delighted to present the work of these three exceptional talents to you in this publication.

The book is a piece of living design tradition: each of the three winners is introduced with essays to provide context, a detailed biography and representative images of their works. There are also extended interviews offering

a fascinating insight into specific projects, conceptual and collaborative working processes, and into research and teaching, with interdisciplinary approaches and an expanded concept of design. All the content was created in close collaboration with the winners.

We are delighted to be launching a revamped Swiss Grand Award for Design book series. Each year, the fascinating combination of three personalities from widely differing fields of activity opens up a new and inspiring perspective on the world of Swiss design.

I should like to take this opportunity to thank Julia Born, Peter Knapp and Sarah Owens as well as the members of the Federal Design Commission, all of whom, through their commitment, have played a vital role in making this book a success. My grateful thanks also go to everyone else involved: the coordinator, designers, authors, translators, photographer and proofreaders.

Anna Niederhäuser
Bundesamt für Kultur
Office fédéral de la culture
Ufficio federale della cultura
Federal Office of Culture

Swiss Grand Award for Design Winners 2007–21

2021
Julia Born
　Graphic designer
Peter Knapp
　Photographer
　and art director
Sarah Owens
　Design educator
　and researcher

2020
Ida Gut
　Fashion designer
Monique Jacot
　Photographer
Kueng Caputo
　Product designers

2019
Rosmarie Baltensweiler
　Product designer
Connie Hüsser
　Interior stylist
Thomi Wolfensberger
　Lithographer and publisher

2018
Cécile Feilchenfeldt
　Textile designer
Felco
　Product design
Rosmarie Tissi
　Graphic designer

2017
David Bielander
　Jewellery designer
Thomas Ott
　Illustrator
Jean Widmer
　Graphic designer
　and art director

2016
Claudia Caviezel
　Textile designer
Hans Eichenberger
　Product and
　interior designer
Ralph Schraivogel
　Graphic designer

2015
Luc Chessex
　Photographer
Lora Lamm
　Graphic designer
Team '77
　Typographers and
　type designers

2014
Erich Biehle
　Textile designer
Alfredo Häberli
　Furniture and
　product designer
Wolfgang Weingart
　Typographer

2013
Trix & Robert Haussmann
　Interior and
　product designers
Armin Hofmann
　Graphic designer
Martin Leuthold
　Textile designer

2012
Franco Clivio
　Product designer
Gavillet & Rust
　Graphic designers
Karl Gerstner
　Graphic designer

2011
Jörg Boner
　Product designer
NORM
　Graphic designers
Ernst Scheidegger
　Photographer
Walter Steiger
　Footwear designer

2010
Susi & Ueli Berger
　Furniture designers
Jean-Luc Godard
　Filmmaker
Sonnhild Kestler
　Textile designer
Otto Künzli
　Jewellery designer

2009
Robert Frank
　Photographer
Christoph Hefti
　Textile designer
Ursula Rodel
　Fashion designer
Thut Möbel
　Furniture design

2008
Holzer Kobler Architekturen
　Exhibition designers
　and architects
Albert Kriemler (Akris)
　Fashion designer
Alain Kupper
　Graphic designer, musician,
　artist and gallery owner
Walter Pfeiffer
　Photographer

2007
Ruth Grüninger
　Fashion designer
NOSE
　Communication design,
　service design
Bernhard Schobinger
　Jewellery designer
Cornel Windlin
　Graphic designer

Swiss Federal Design Commission 2020–21

Chair
Jörg Boner
　Product designer, Zurich

Members
Claudia Caviezel
　Textile designer, St. Gallen
Marietta Eugster
　Graphic designer, Paris
Davide Fornari
　Associate professor,
　Research and Development,
　ECAL, Renens
Tatyana Franck
　Director, Musée de l'Elysée,
　Lausanne
Aude Lehmann
　Graphic designer, Zurich
Vera Sacchetti
　Design critic and curator,
　Basel

Colophon

Published on the occasion
of the Swiss Grand Award
for Design 2021

Head of project
　Anna Niederhäuser
　Federal Office of Culture
　(FOC), Bern
Editing, project coordination
　Mirjam Fischer, mille pages,
　Zurich
Art direction and design
　Ard – Guillaume Chuard
　& Daniel Kang Yoon
　Nørregaard,
　London/Lausanne
Typeface
　RH Geigy, Robert Huber,
　Zurich
Photography
　© FOC/Diana Pfammatter
　(p. 10, 17, 46, 53, 82, 89)
Interviews and texts
　Angie Keefer and David
　Bennewith (Julia Born)
　Tatyana Franck and
　François Cheval
　(Peter Knapp)
　Vera Sacchetti and Jonas
　Berthod (Sarah Owens)
Editing
　Audrey Hoareau
　(conversation Tatyana
　Franck and Peter Knapp)
Translations
　Geoff Spearing (E)
　Tan Wälchli (D – Julia Born)
　FOC Translation
　Services (D/F/I)
Proofreading
　FOC Translation
　Services (D/F/I)
　Geoff Spearing (E)
Colours separation
　DL Imaging, London
Printing
　Gremper AG, Basel

Weitere Übersetzungen der
　Interviews finden Sie auf:
Veuillez trouver les traductions
　françaises sur :
La traduzione italiana delle
　interviste è disponibile su:
www.schweizerkulturpreise.ch/
design

© 2021 the authors, artists,
FOC and Verlag Scheidegger
& Spiess AG, Zürich
© for the texts: the authors
© for the images: the artists

Verlag Scheidegger & Spiess
Niederdorfstrasse 54
8001 Zurich, Switzerland
www.scheidegger-spiess.ch

Scheidegger & Spiess is being
supported by the Federal
Office of Culture with a general
subsidy for the years 2021–24.

All rights reserved; no part
of this publication may be
reproduced, stored in a
retrieval system or transmitted
in any form or by any means,
electronic, mechanical,
photocopying, recording,
or otherwise, without
the prior written consent
of the publisher.

978-3-03942-054-4

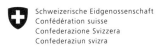

Schweizerische Eidgenossenschaft Eidgenössisches Departement des Innern EDI
Confédération suisse   Département fédéral de l'intérieur DFI
Confederazione Svizzera   Dipartimento federale dell'interno DFI
Confederaziun svizra   Departament federal da l'intern DFI
                                 Bundesamt für Kultur BAK
                                 Office fédéral de la culture OFC
                                 Ufficio federale della cultura UFC
                                 Uffizi federal da cultura UFC

Julia Born

Grafikdesignerin

Designer graphique   Designer grafica

Graphic Designer

Julia Born holding *Michel Auder. Stories, Myths, Ironies, and Other Songs*, silkscreen poster for Kunsthalle Basel, photographed by Diana Pfammatter, Zurich, 17 May 2021

Julia Born   Angleichung & Justierung   von David Bennewith

Sollten Sie jemals in die Situation kommen, einem Kind – wahrscheinlich im Zusammenhang mit irgendeiner manuellen Operation – den Unterschied zwischen einer Angleichung[1] und einer Justierung[2] erklären zu müssen, werden Sie vermutlich ein Gelächter auslösen. Ein auf gegenseitiges Verständnis abzielender Prozess kann als Angleichung bezeichnet werden – sie erlaubt es, auch zahllose Elemente des Kontexts ins Verständnis mit einzubeziehen. Gewöhnlich führt ein solcher Prozess irgendwann zu einem Konsens, und dies eröffnet ein Feld für letzte Justierungen und schliesslich für eine Festlegung, einen Abdruck. Die Praxis des Grafikdesigns verlangt es, immer wieder zwischen diesen zwei Grenzbereichen – Angleichung und Justierung – hin und her zu wechseln. Sich die Bewegung auch nur ansatzweise vor Augen zu halten, reizt sofort zum Lachen.

Als Angleichung kann auch das gegenseitige Verständnis bezeichnet werden, das auf das Resultat hinauslief, dass Julia Born den Grand Prix Swiss Design erhielt. Das Folgende sind die Justierungen dieser Angleichung.

Eine Standard-Justierung:

Julia Born lebt und arbeitet in Zürich. Seit sie im Jahr 2000 ihr Studium an der Gerrit Rietveld Academie in Amsterdam abschloss, war sie in vielfältige Projekte zwischen der Schweiz, Amsterdam und Berlin involviert. Schwerpunkt ihrer Arbeit ist Editorial Design für Institutionen aus dem Kulturbereich: Stedelijk Museum und Rijksakademie Amsterdam, Kunsthalle Basel, ICA Miami, Guggenheim Museum New York, Hamburger Bahnhof, HKW, Brücke-Museum Berlin und die documenta 14 in Kassel und Athen. Im engen Dialog mit Institutionen, freischaffenden Kuratorinnen und Kuratoren sowie Kunstschaffenden entstanden so Publikationen, Visuelle Identitäten, Ausstellungsdesign und vieles mehr. Neben den Auftragsarbeiten beteiligte sich Julia Born immer wieder an freieren und oft investigativ ausgerichteten Kollaborationen, unter anderem mit der Fotografin Uta Eisenreich, dem Modedesigner JOFF und der Performancekünstlerin Alexandra Bachzetsis. Diese Projekte drehen sich um Fragestellungen des Sprachgebrauchs und der Repräsentation. Julia Born unterrichtet Grafikdesign an der Gerrit Rietveld Academie in Amsterdam und an der École cantonale d'art de Lausanne (ECAL). Als Gastdozentin wirkt sie u.a. an der Yale School of Arts, der Rhode Island School of Design (RISD), der University of Seoul, dem CCA San Francisco sowie am Werkplaats Typografie in Arnheim. Von 2003 bis 2007 war sie Jurymitglied des Wettbewerbs «Die Schönsten Schweizer Bücher». Anlässlich des Inform-Preises für konzeptionelles Gestalten realisierte sie ihre erste Einzelausstellung und den Katalog *Title of the Show* in der Galerie für Zeitgenössische Kunst Leipzig. Sie erhielt unter anderem den Charlotte-Köhler-Preis 2008, den Jan-Tschichold-Preis 2011 und den Schweizer Designpreis 2003, 2007 und 2018.

Hey Kids! Wollen wir nicht doch lieber die Angleichung beschreiben? Vielleicht geht's doch eher darum:

Bei den (Pfad-)Finderinnen mitmachen [diese ganz besondere Idee von Dienstleistung, Struktur und Freiheit, die sowohl Angleichungen innerhalb der Hierarchien als auch dagegen hervorbringt]. Durch die Eltern und mit ihnen Kunst und Design kennenlernen. Mit den Büchern auf ihren Regalen aufwachsen – das Schnipseln und Schneiden, die Löcher, Farben und Materialien, die in entschiedener und finaler Ordnung erscheinen. *Their Finite Bliss*. Eine Mathelehrerin am Gymnasium, eine politisch bewanderte, engagierte Feministin mit Migrationshintergrund. Ein Nebenjob in einer Zürcher Frucht- und Gemüsehandlung (wo die Besitzerin ihr Dinge fürs Leben beibrachte) und wo sie gelegentlich die verfaulenden Restbestände fotografierte, um Bilder für die Bewerbung an der Kunsthochschule zu haben. Dort angekommen, eine ganze Litanei von nicht-linearen und trans-disziplinären Verbindungen anhören, auch konzeptionelles Denken und Überlegungen zu Archiven sowie absurde Aufgabestellungen (basierend auf dem beliebtesten Gemüse der Niederlande). Es gab damals viele 'uncoole' und 'unkuratierte' Aufgaben. Lernen, aus fast nichts wenigstens irgendetwas zu machen – aus einer blossen Frage oder nur einer Laune von Dozierenden. *Looser Times*. Die guten Dozierenden, und sogar die schlechten, und dann trotzdem selbst Dozentin werden, gleich nach dem Abschluss! Als solche sich immer Zeit nehmen, mit dem arbeiten, was an den Tisch gebracht wird, und nie eine Diskussion verlassen, ohne etwas beigetragen zu haben. *Late Evenings and Nights*. Lehre und

---

1. Im Original engl. alignment, heisst auch z. B. Ausrichtung (beim Textsatz), Anordnung, Harmonisierung.
2. Im Original engl. registration, heisst auch z. B. Registrierung (beim Druck), Eintragung, Zulassung.

Praxis sind immer verbunden. Die Schule ist ein spezieller Ort, aber das Studio auch. *Fear, Courage, Feeling, Scent, Touch, Love. Babe.* Eine tiefgründige und anspruchsvolle Kollaborateurin, eine Entscheidungsträgerin, immer im Hinblick auf die Überlegungen von anderen. Das vierteljährliche Programm der (Pfad-)Finderinnen, die Fanzines und Telefonlisten, in Briefen an die Eltern verschiedene Unterschriften ausprobieren ... So hat das mit dem Grafikdesign angefangen.*

Vielleicht könnte man sagen: Die Justierung verrät die Seele, aber die Angleichung begehrt sie.

* Angleichungen in der Reihenfolge ihres Erscheinens: (Pfad-)Finderinnen, Eltern, *ACID. Neue amerikanische Szene*, herausgegeben von R.D. Brinkmann und R.R. Rygulla, März Verlag, Darmstadt 1969; *Markus Raetz 1986*, Kunsthaus Zürich; *Schnippelbuch*; Helen Faigle, Loris Scola; René van der Land, Giene Steenman und Hewald Jongenelis (Gerrit Rietveld Academie, Basisjaar), Linda van Deursen, Frans Oosterhof und *gestrichen* (Gerrit Rietveld Academie, Grafikdesign), diverse Schulen, Studierende, Mitarbeitende sowie Auftraggeberinnen und Auftraggeber und so weiter.

Julia Born   Alignement & réglage   par David Bennewith

S'il vous arrivait de devoir expliquer à un enfant – en particulier autour de certaines manipulations – la différence entre un alignement[1] et un réglage[2], il y aura certainement de quoi rire. Un processus visant à un accord mutuel peut être considéré comme un alignement – il permet d'intégrer le contexte et sa myriade d'éléments. Ce processus aboutira finalement à un consensus et débouchera sur un champ pour le réglage, puis sur le tirage. Dans son travail, un designer graphique évolue souvent entre ces deux espaces liminaux – alignement et réglage. S'imaginer brièvement ce va-et-vient peut faire sourire.

L'accord mutuel débouchant sur l'attribution de ce prix à Julia Born est un alignement. Ce qui suit, et l'entoure, constitue les réglages de cet alignement.

Un réglage standard :

Julia Born vit et travaille à Zurich. Après avoir achevé ses études à la Gerrit Rietveld Academie d'Amsterdam en 2000, elle a travaillé sur différents projets entre la Suisse, Amsterdam et Berlin. Son travail se concentre sur le design éditorial pour des clients du monde culturel tels que le Stedelijk Museum ou l'Académie royale des beaux-arts d'Amsterdam, la Kunsthalle de Bâle, l'ICA Miami, le musée Solomon R. Guggenheim de New York, la Maison des cultures du monde, le Brücke-Museum et la Hamburger Bahnhof de Berlin ou la documenta 14 de Cassel et d'Athènes. Ce travail, développé en contact étroit avec les institutions, les curateurs et les artistes, inclut des publications, des identités visuelles, le design d'expositions et bien plus. À côté de ses mandats, elle a régulièrement collaboré à des projets de recherche avec d'autres designers et artistes tels que la photographe Uta Eisenreich, le designer de mode JOFF et l'artiste chorégraphe Alexandra Bachzetsis. Ces projets tournent autour de la question du langage et de la représentation. Julia enseigne régulièrement le design graphique à la Gerrit Rietveld Academie d'Amsterdam et à l'ECAL, l'École cantonale d'art de Lausanne, et est conférencière invitée dans différentes institutions d'enseignement du design et de l'art, en particulier la Yale School of Arts, la RISD Rhode Island School of Design, l'Université de Séoul, le CCA à San Francisco et le Werkplaats Typografie d'Arnhem. De 2003 à 2007, elle a été membre du jury du concours « Les plus beaux livres suisses ». À l'occasion de l'Inform Award for Conceptual Design, elle a produit sa première exposition individuelle et le catalogue *Title of the Show* à la Galerie für Zeitgenössische Kunst Leipzig. Entre autres prix, elle a reçu le Charlotte Köhler Prijs en 2008, le Prix Jan Tschichold en 2011 et un Prix suisse du design en 2003, 2007 et 2018.

Hé les enfants ! Peut-on dire quelque chose sur l'alignement ? C'est peut-être ça l'essentiel ? :

Être scout(e) [*cette* idée bien particulière de service, de structure et de liberté qui produit à la fois des alignements au sein et à l'encontre de ses hiérarchies]. Découvrir l'art et le design par et avec ses parents. Grandir avec ces livres sur leurs étagères – les découpages, les coupures, les trous, les couleurs et les matériaux ; faits, arrangés et produits dans un ordre précis et finalisé. *Their Finite Bliss*. Une prof de maths au gymnase, féministe engagée, cultivée en politique et fille d'une famille d'immigrants. Travail à temps partiel dans un magasin de fruits et légumes à Zurich (où la propriétaire lui a appris les choses de la vie) et saisissant l'occasion de photographier les produits en décomposition pour son dossier d'inscription à l'école d'art. Et là,

1.   Dans la version originale anglaise alignment peut signifier également p.ex. synchronisation, ajustement, calibration.
2.   Dans la version originale anglaise registration peut signifier également p.ex. montage (en impression), enregistrement, inscription.

rencontre avec une litanie de relations non linéaires et trans-disciplinaires, de pensées conceptuelles et de considérations archivistiques, des exercices absurdes (autour du légume le plus populaire de Hollande), à l'époque, un tas de travaux 'pas cools' et 'pas curatés'. Apprendre à faire quelque chose à partir de presque rien, la question ou le caprice d'un professeur. *Looser Times.* Les bons profs et même les mauvais, pour ensuite devenir elle-même professeure – juste après le diplôme – rien de moins! Une professeure qui prend toujours le temps, qui travaille avec ce qui est là et ne quitte jamais une discussion sans avoir donné quelque chose. *Late Evening and Nights.* L'enseignement et la pratique sont toujours connectés. L'école est un lieu spécial, comme l'atelier. *Fear, Courage, Feeling, Scent, Touch, Love. Babe.* Une collaboratrice experimentée et exigeante, une décideuse, attentive aux réflexions des autres. Le programme trimestriel des scout(e)s, les fanzines, les listes de téléphone, essayant différentes signatures dans les lettres aux parents... C'est ainsi qu'elle a fait ses premiers pas dans le design graphique! *

Hypothèse : le réglage estompe l'âme, l'alignement la désire.

* Alignement par ordre d'apparition : scout(e)s, parents, *ACID. Neue amerikanische Szene,* édité par R.D. Brinkmann et R.R. Rygulla, publié par Darmstadt, März Verlag, 1969; *Markus Raetz 1986,* Kunsthaus Zürich; *Schnippelbuch* (livre d'archives d'images); Helen Faigle, Loris Scola; René van der Land, Giene Steenman et Hewald Jongenelis (Gerrit Rietveld Academie, Basisjaar), Linda van Deursen, Frans Oosterhof et *supprimé* (Gerrit Rietveld Academie, Graphic design); différentes écoles, différent.e.s étudiant.e.s, collaborateur.trice.s et commissaires; à suivre.

Julia Born   Allineamento & registro   di David Bennewith

Se si dovesse spiegare a un bambino, in genere nel contesto di un qualche tipo di operazione manuale, la differenza fra allineamento[1] e registro[2], probabilmente si metterebbe a ridere. Un processo che porta a un accordo reciproco può essere definito allineamento, poiché permette una comprensione del contesto e della miriade di elementi che lo compongono. Il processo per raggiungere questa comprensione reciproca porta infine a un consenso, il cui risultato è uno spazio per il registro e la produzione di un'impressione. Un progettista grafico si muove spesso fra questi spazi liminali – di allineamento e di registro – nella propria pratica professionale. Il solo accennare a immaginare questo movimento potrebbe risultare comico.

L'accordo reciproco che ha portato come risultato l'assegnazione di questo premio a Julia Born è un allineamento. Quel che segue e circonda quest'accordo sono le sue registrazioni.

Un tipo di registrazione standard:

Julia Born vive e lavora a Zurigo. Dopo aver completato gli studi alla Gerrit Rietveld Academie di Amsterdam nel 2000, ha lavorato a vari progetti fra la Svizzera, Amsterdam e Berlino. Il suo lavoro si concentra su progetti editoriali per svariati operatori culturali come lo Stedelijk Museum o la Rijksakademie di Amsterdam, la Kunsthalle di Basilea, l'ICA di Miami, il Guggenheim Museum di New York, la Hamburger Bahnhof, HKW, il Brücke-Museum di Berlino o la documenta 14 a Kassel e ad Atene. I suoi lavori – sviluppati in stretta collaborazione con le istituzioni, i curatori e gli artisti – includono pubblicazioni, progetti di identità, allestimenti di mostre e altro. Oltre ai suoi incarichi su commissione, ha partecipato costantemente a progetti di ricerca riguardo il linguaggio e la rappresentazione, in collaborazione con altri designer e artisti, tra cui la fotografa Uta Eisenreich, il fashion designer JOFF e l'artista performativa Alexandra Bachzetsis. Julia Born insegna design grafico alla Gerrit Rietveld Academie di Amsterdam e all'ECAL, École cantonale d'art de Lausanne, ed è docente ospite in vari istituti d'arte e di design, tra cui la Yale School of Arts, la Rhode Island School of Design (RISD), la University of Seoul, il CCA di San Francisco e la Werkplaats Typografie di Arnhem. È stata membro della giuria del concorso «I più bei libri svizzeri» dal 2003 al 2007. In occasione del premio Inform per il design concettuale, ha realizzato la sua prima mostra personale e il catalogo *Title of the Show* al Galerie für Zeitgenössische Kunst Leipzig in Germania. Ha ricevuto tra l'altro il premio Charlotte Köhler nel 2008, il premio Jan Tschichold nel 2011 e il Premio svizzero di design negli anni 2003, 2007 e 2018.

Ehi ragazzi! Possiamo scrivere qualcosa sull'allineamento? ... Forse è proprio questo il punto?:

Essere una (ragazza) scout [*quel* particolare senso di impegno, struttura e libertà che crea al contempo allineamento all'interno delle gerarchie e contro di esse]. Entrare in contatto con l'arte e il design

1. Nella versione originale inglese alignment può essere inteso, ad esempio, come allineamento, calibratura, sincronizzazione.
2. Nella versione originale inglese registration può essere inteso, ad esempio, come messa a registro (nella stampa), registrazione, iscrizione.

insieme e attraverso i propri genitori. Crescere con i libri sui loro scaffali – sforbiciando, tagliando, bucherellando, usando colori e materiali diversi; il tutto fatto, sistemato e creato secondo un ordine ben preciso e finito. *Their Finite Bliss*. Una professoressa di matematica delle superiori, informata sulla politica, femminista impegnata e figlia di una famiglia di immigrati. Un lavoro part-time da un fruttivendolo di Zurigo (dove la proprietaria le ha insegnato le cose della *vita*) e dove nei ritagli di tempo fotografava gli ortaggi deperiti per il portfolio del concorso di ammissione alla scuola d'arte. Una volta entrata, imbattersi in una pletora di connessioni non-lineari e transdisciplinari, ragionamenti concettuali e riflessioni sull'archivio, temi di progetto assurdi (basati sulla *più amata* verdura d'Olanda), un sacco di temi di progetto poco *cool* e «non curati», a quei tempi. Imparare a fare qualcosa a partire da quasi niente, basandosi solo sulla domanda o il capriccio di un docente. *Looser Times*. I docenti bravi e persino quelli cattivi. E poi essere invitata a diventare docente – subito dopo il diploma – niente meno! Da docente: prendersi sempre il tempo, lavorare con quel che c'è a disposizione, senza mai abbandonare una discussione senza aver dato *qualcosa*. *Late Evenings and Nights*. Insegnamento e pratica professionale sono sempre connessi. La scuola è un luogo speciale, come anche lo studio. *Fear, Courage, Feeling, Scent, Touch, Love. Babe.* Una collaboratrice profonda ed esigente, che sa prendere decisioni tenendo conto delle considerazioni altrui. Il Programma Trimestrale per (ragazze) scout, le fanzine e le rubriche telefoniche, esercitarsi sulle diverse firme nelle lettere ai genitori... questi sono i suoi primi esperimenti di progettazione grafica.*

Forse: la messa a registro cela l'anima, e l'allineamento la desidera.

* Allineamenti in ordine di apparizione: (ragazze) scout, genitori, *ACID. Neue amerikanische Szene*, a cura di R.D. Brinkmann e R.R. Rygulla, edito a Darmstadt, März Verlag, 1969; *Markus Raetz 1986*, Kunsthaus Zürich; *Schnippelbuch* (Libro di ritagli); Helen Faigle, Loris Scola; René van der Land, Giene Steenman e Hewald Jongenelis (Gerrit Rietveld Academie, Basisjaar), Linda van Deursen, Frans Oosterhof e *omissis* (Gerrit Rietveld Academie, Graphic design), varie scuole, svariati studenti, collaboratori e clienti; e così via.

Julia Born Alignment & Registration by David Bennewith

If you ever happen to have to explain to a kid – usually in connection with some kind of a manual operation – the difference between alignment and registration, they will likely laugh. A process towards a mutual understanding can be referred to as alignment – it allows for an understanding of the context and its myriad elements. This process of finding mutual understanding eventually leads to a consensus, resulting in a field for registration and the making of an impression. A graphic designer often moves between these liminal spaces – of alignment and registration – in their practice. Even a cursory imagination of this movement might induce laughter.

The mutual understanding that has led to the result of Julia Born receiving this award is an alignment. That which follows, and surrounds, is its registrations.

A standard kind of registration:

Julia Born lives and works in Zurich. After completing her studies at Amsterdam's Gerrit Rietveld Academie in 2000, she worked on various projects between Switzerland, Amsterdam and Berlin. Her work focuses on editorial design for a variety of cultural clients such as the Stedelijk Museum and the Rijksakademie in Amsterdam, Kunsthalle Basel, ICA Miami, Guggenheim Museum New York, Hamburger Bahnhof, HKW and Brücke-Museum in Berlin, and documenta 14 in Kassel and Athens. The work, developed in close dialogue with institutions, curators and artists, includes publications, identities, exhibition design and more. Apart from commissioned work she has continually collaborated with other designers and artists on investigative projects, with – among others – photographer Uta Eisenreich, fashion designer JOFF, and performance artist Alexandra Bachzetsis. These projects revolve around the subject of language and representation. Julia regularly teaches graphic design at the Gerrit Rietveld Academie in Amsterdam and ECAL, École cantonale d'art de Lausanne, and is a visiting lecturer at international art and design institutes, among others the Yale School of Arts, RISD Rhode Island School of Design, the University of Seoul, CCA San Francisco and Werkplaats Typografie in Arnhem. From 2003 to 2007 she was a jury member of the "Most Beautiful Swiss Books" competition. On the occasion of the Inform Award for Conceptual Design, she produced her first solo show and the catalogue *Title of the Show*, at the Galerie für Zeitgenössische Kunst Leipzig, Germany. Among other prizes she received the Charlotte Köhler Prijs in 2008, the Jan Tschichold Prize in 2011, and the Swiss Design Award in 2003, 2007 and 2018.

Hey kids! Can we write about the alignment? ... Perhaps that's where it's really at?:

Being a (Girl)Scout [*that* particular notion of service, structure and freedom that creates alignments both within and against its hierarchies]. Being exposed to art and design with and through her parents. Growing up with the books on their shelves – the snipping, cutting, holes, colours and materials; made, arranged and produced in a decisive and finite order. Their Finite Bliss. A high-school math teacher, a politically literate, engaged feminist and daughter of an immigrant family. A part-time job in a Zurich fruit and veg store (where the owner taught her about *life*) and, then and there, photographing its decaying produce to make images in order to enter art school. At art school, encountering a litany of non-linear and trans-disciplinary connections, conceptual thinking and archival considerations, absurd assignments (based around *the most* popular vegetable in Holland), lots of 'uncool' and 'un-curated' assignments back then. Learning to make something from nothing much, only from a teacher's question or whim. Looser Times. The good teachers and even the bad teachers, and then being asked to be a teacher – right after graduation – no less! As a teacher always taking the time, working with what is brought to the table, and never leaving the discussion without giving *something*. Late Evenings and Nights. Teaching and practice are always connected. School is a special place, as is the studio. Fear, Courage, Feeling, Scent, Touch, Love. Babe. A deep and demanding collaborator, a decision maker, towards the deliberations of others. The Quarterly Programme for the (Girl)Scouts, the fanzines and phone lists, trying out different signatures in letters to the parents ... this is where she first did graphic design!*

Maybe: Registration belies soul, and Alignment desires it.

* Alignments in order of appearance: (girl)scouts, parents, *ACID. Neue amerikanische Szene*, edited by R.D. Brinkmann and R.R. Rygulla, published by März Verlag, Darmstadt, 1969; *Markus Raetz 1986*, Kunsthaus Zürich; *Schnippelbuch* (Clippings Book); Helen Faigle, Loris Scola; René van der Land, Giene Steenman and Hewald Jongenelis (Gerrit Rietveld Academie, Basic Year), Linda van Deursen, Frans Oosterhof and *redacted* (Gerrit Rietveld Academie, Graphic design), various schools, various students, collaborators and commissioners, onwards.

David Bennewith
Leiter Grafik Design, Gerrit Rietveld Academie, Amsterdam (NL)
Responsable Design Graphique, Gerrit Rietveld Academie, Amsterdam (NL)
Responsabile graphic design, Gerrit Rietveld Academie, Amsterdam (NL)
Head of graphic design, Gerrit Rietveld Academie, Amsterdam (NL)

Julia Born

1975 born in Zurich
since 2016 based in Zurich
2012–16 based in Berlin (DE)
1996–2012 based in Amsterdam (NL)

Education

1996–2000 Basisjaar and Graphic Design (BA), Gerrit Rietveld Academie, Amsterdam (NL)
1990–95 Liceo Artistico, Zurich

Awards & grants

2018/07/03 Swiss Federal Design Award, Swiss Federal Office of Culture
2012 Praktijksubsidie, Mondriaan Fonds, Amsterdam (NL)
2011 Jan Tschichold Prize, Swiss Federal Office of Culture
2009 Inform Prize for Conceptual Design, Galerie für Zeitgenössische Kunst, Leipzig (DE)
2008 Charlotte Köhler Prijs, Prins Bernhard Cultuurfonds, Amsterdam (NL)
2004 Werkbeitrag, Swiss Federal Office of Culture
2000 Frans de Jongprijs, Den Haag (NL)

Teaching

since 2018 Master Type Design, ECAL École cantonale d'art de Lausanne
since 2014 Rietveld Berlin/Zurich, with Laurenz Brunner, Gerrit Rietveld Academie, Amsterdam (NL)
2008/10/13 Visiting lecturer, Yale University School of Art, New Haven (USA)
since 2003 Graphic Design department, Gerrit Rietveld Academie, Amsterdam (NL)
2002 Teacher, BA Graphic Design, ECAL École cantonale d'art de Lausanne

Workshops, lectures, symposia

since 2002 Art Center College of Design, Los Angeles/CA (USA); CalArts, Santa Clarita/CA (USA); Centre culturel suisse, Paris (FR); Centro Carioca de Design, Rio de Janeiro (BR); Chaumont Poster Festival, Chaumont (FR); CNEAI Paris (FR); CCA/CRB, California College of the Arts / Curatorial Research Bureau, San Francisco (USA); ECAL, Lausanne; EESAB École européenne supérieure d'art de Bretagne, Rennes (FR); ENSBA École nationale des beaux-arts de Lyon, Lyon (FR); Estonian Academy of Arts, Tallinn (EE); Form Design Center, Malmö (SE); HfG Hochschule für Gestaltung, Karlsruhe (DE); HGB Hochschule für Grafik und Buchkunst, Leipzig (DE); IASPIS, Stockholm (SE); Konstfack, Stockholm; Jan van Eyck Academie, Maastricht (NL); KASK, Gent (BE); Kunstnernes Hus, Oslo (NO); Officin, Copenhagen (DK); REDO Design Conference, Priština (XK); RISD Rhode Island School of Design, Providence (USA); SfG Schule für Gestaltung, Basel; Sint Lucas, Gent (BE); The Academy of Arts, Architecture and Design, Prague (CZ); University of Seoul, Seoul (KOR); Werkplaats Typografie, Arnhem (NL); Yale University School of Art, New Haven (USA); ZHdK Zürcher Hochschule der Künste, Zurich

Exhibitions (selection)

2020 *Dance First Think Later*, Le Commun, Bâtiment d'art contemporain (BAC), Geneva, with Alexandra Bachzetsis, curated by Olivier Kaeser
2017 *Soil Erosion*, San Francisco (USA), with Alexandra Bachzetsis, curated by Shannon Ebner, Altman Siegel
2012–14 *Graphic Design: Now in Production*, Walker Art Center, Minneapolis (USA), Cooper-Hewitt, National Design Museum, curated by Ian Albinson, Ellen Lupton et al.
2011 *The Way Beyond Art: Wide White Space*, CCA Wattis Institute for Contemporary Arts, San Francisco (USA), curated by Jon Sueda
2010 *Performative Structures*, Alte Fabrik Rapperswil, with Alexandra Bachzetsis, curated by Alexandra Blättler
2009 *Julia Born. Title of the Show*, Galerie für Zeitgenössische Kunst, Leipzig (DE), solo show in collaboration with Laurenz Brunner
2009 *Quick, Quick, Slow*, Experimenta Lisbon (PT), curated by Emily King
2008 *Word Event*, Kunsthalle Basel, with Alexandra Bachzetsis, curated by Maxine Kopsa and Roos Gortzak
2007 *Forms of Inquiry*, AA London (UK), with Alexandra Bachzetsis, curated by Zak Kyes

2006 *Graphic Design in the White Cube*, Graphic Design Biennale, Brno/CZ, curated by Peter Bil'ak

2005 *Dutch Resource,* Chaumont Poster Festival, Chaumont (FR), organised by Werkplaats Typografie

2005 *Cool School*, Gallery of The Academy of Arts, Architecture and Design, Prague (CZ), curated by Adam Macháček and Radim Peško

2004 *Work from Switzerland*, Moravian Gallery, Brno/CZ

2004 *Mark,* Municipal Acquisitions, Stedelijk Museum Amsterdam (NL)

2003 *Invitation N°75,* Stedelijk Museum Bureau Amsterdam (NL), with JOFF and Corriette Schoenarts, curated by Bart van der Heide

Collections and archives

Stedelijk Museum Amsterdam (NL)
Graphics Collection and Poster Collection, Museum für Gestaltung Zürich

Long-term collaborators

Alexandra Bachzetsis, artist, choreographer, Zurich
Laurenz Brunner, graphic designer, type designer, Zurich
Uta Eisenreich, artist, Amsterdam (NL)
Linda van Deursen, graphic designer, educator, Amsterdam (NL)
JOFF, fashion designer, educator, New York (USA)
Adam Szymczyk, curator, writer, Zurich

Artists, assistants, commissioners, co-teachers, curators, designers, editors, photographers, printers, publishers

since 1999 Igshaan Adams, Cape Town; Marina Arnoldt, DZA Druckerei zu Altenburg GmbH, Altenburg; Michel Auder, New York; David Bennewith, Amsterdam; Jennifer Blessing, Guggenheim Museum, New York; Blommers/Schumm, Amsterdam; Franziska Born, Zurich; Klaus Born, Dietlikon; Boyplaygirl, Brita Lindvall & Robin Ekemark, Stockholm; Binna Choi, Casco – Office for Art, Design and Theory, Utrecht; Patrizia Crivelli, FOC Bern; Moyra Davey, New York; Shannon Ebner, Los Angeles/New York; Martin Eicher, asa AG, Rapperswil/Jona; Elektrosmog, Valentin Hindermann & Marco Walser, Zurich; Fanni Fetzer, Kunstmuseum Luzern; Mirjam Fischer, FOC Bern, mille pages, Zurich; Hendrik Folkerts, Art Institute of Chicago; Anselm Franke & Eyal Weizman, Haus der Kulturen der Welt, Berlin, Forensic Architecture, London; Alex Gartenfeld, ICA Miami; Sam de Groot, Amsterdam; Joyce Guley, Knust/Extrapool, Nijmegen; Hanne Hagenaars for Museum Boijmans van Beuningen, Rotterdam; Melanie Hofmann, Zurich; Daria Holme, Mannheim; Xander Karskens, Amsterdam; Angie Keefer, Hudson/NY; Jean Bernard Koeman, W139, Amsterdam; Freek Kuin, drukkerij Calff & Meischke, robstolk, Amsterdam; Quinn Latimer, documenta 14, Kassel/Athens; Aude Lehmann, Zurich; Alon Levin, Berlin; Kees Maas, Amsterdam; Anna Manubens, CA2M Madrid; Metzger Zimmermann de Perrot, Zurich; Adeline Mollard, Zurich; Julia Novitch, Berlin; Marina Olsen & Karolina Dankow, Karma International, Zurich; Domeniek Ruyters, Metropolis M, Utrecht; Scheltens & Abbenes, Amsterdam; Lisa Marei Schmidt, Hamburger Bahnhof, Berlin, Brücke-Museum, Berlin; Maaike Schoorel, Amsterdam; Ferdi Sieben, TNT Post, Den Haag; Studio Moniker, Amsterdam; Wendelien van Oldenborgh, Rotterdam/Berlin; Nina Paim, Basel; Emily Pethick, Casco, Utrecht, Rijksakademie voor beeldende kunsten, Amsterdam; Andreas Pöge, Pöge Druck, Leipzig; Mark-Emil Poulsen, Copenhagen; Paul B. Preciado, documenta 14, Kassel/Athens; Christina Reble, Museum für Gestaltung Zürich; Sereina Rothenberger, Zurich; Johannes Schwartz, Amsterdam; Vivian Suter, Panajachel; Anne-Sofie Thomsen, Copenhagen; Nicolas Trembley, CCS Paris; Lex Trüb, Zurich; Esther Hemmes, Stedelijk Museum Amsterdam; Eva Wagner, Präsidialdepartement der Stadt Zürich; Jan Wenzel, Spector Books Leipzig; Lisa Pepita Weiss, Berlin; Elisabeth Wild, Panajachel, Roger Willems, Roma publications, Amsterdam; Andrzej Wirth, Berlin/Miami, Maja Wismer, Kunstmuseum Basel; Paul Wyber, WyberZeefdruk, Amsterdam

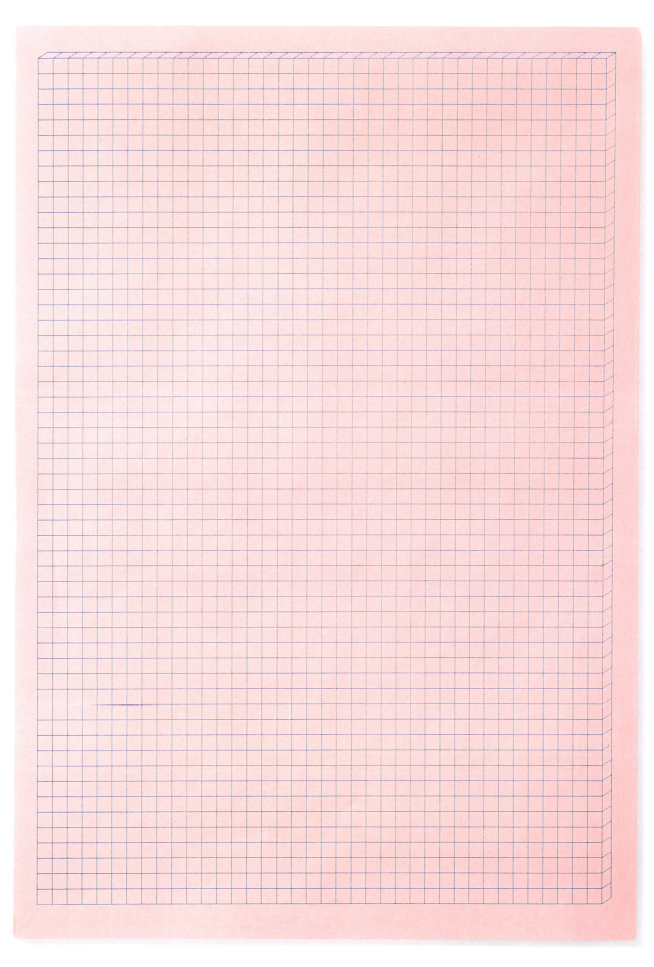

A

SPEAKER

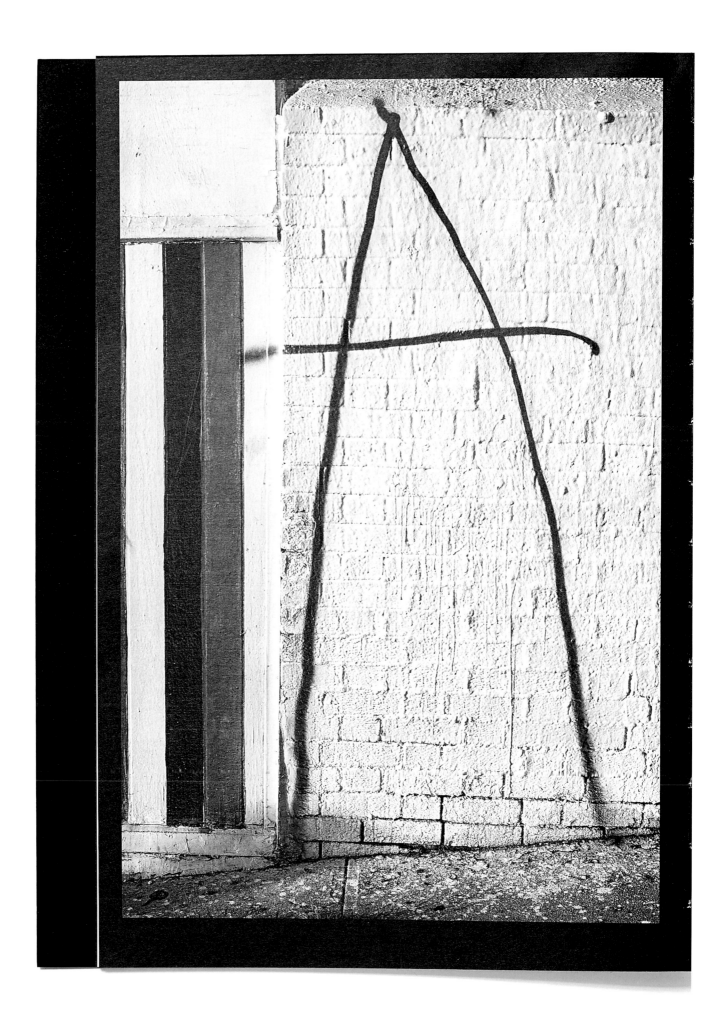

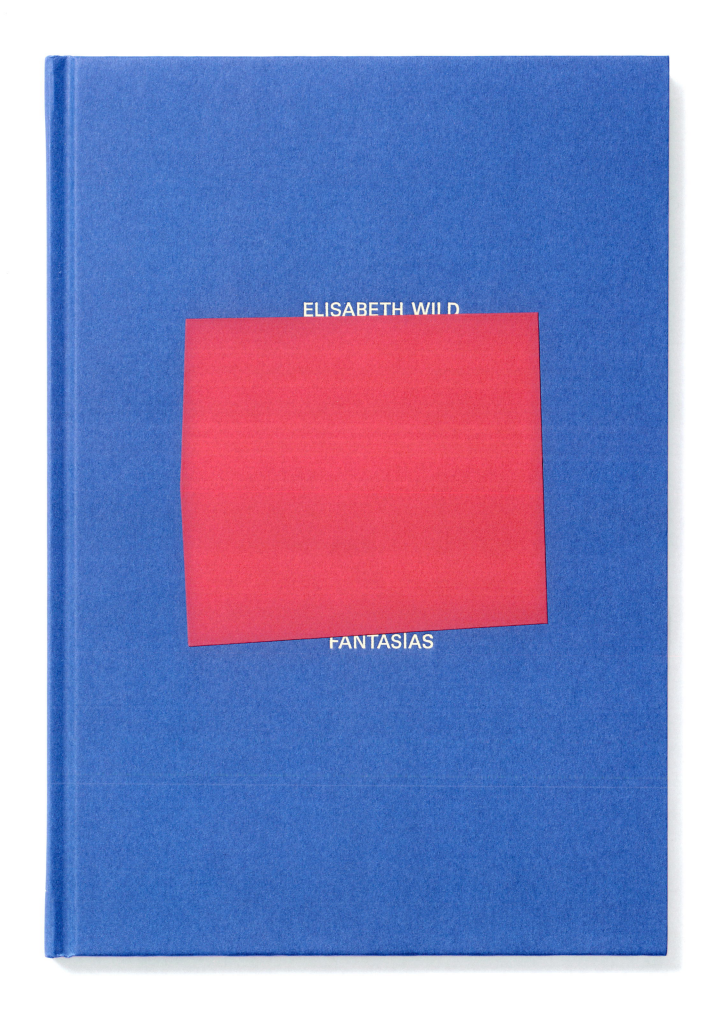

18

19

Offshoot, 2008
Contribution for *A La Mode – ... of Fashion*, page 96–97
In collaboration with JOFF and Blommers/...

Ofoffjoff – One To One, 2007
Publication, 23 × 31 cm, page 144–145
Offset print
In collaboration with JOFF and Blommers/Sch...

1 2 3 4 5 6 7 8 9 10 11 12 13 14 15 16 17 18 19 20 30 40

Link

Voorstel tot Gemeentelijke
Kunstaankopen Fotografie
2002–2003

Proposal for
Municipal Acquisitions
Photography 2002–2003

Stedelijk Museum
Amsterdam

cat. N° 875

RECEIVER

A.   Notepad, edition of 100. Part of graduation project, Gerrit Rietveld Academie, 2000
B.   Moyra Davey. *Speaker Receiver*, edited by Adam Szymczyk, Sternberg Press, 2010, cover
C.   Shannon Ebner. *A Public Character*, ICA Miami, Roma Publications, 2016, spread
D.   Alexandra Bachzetsis. *An Ideal for Living*, photography: Blommers/Schumm, insert: Paul B. Preciado; Centre culturel suisse Paris, 2018, spread and insert
E.   Elisabeth Wild. *Fantasías*, edited by Adam Szymczyk, Sternberg Press, 2020, cover
F.   *Julia Born. Title of the Show*, Galerie für Zeitgenössische Kunst, Leipzig, 2009, in collaboration with Laurenz Brunner. Exhibition view © Stefan Fischer
G.   *Matches 1–40*, poster, edition of 30, 84 × 110 cm, silkscreen print
H.   documenta 14 Athens/Kassel, poster, in collaboration with Laurenz Brunner, series of 4 posters, as part of the visual identity, 2014–17
I.   *Link. Proposal for Municipal Acquisitions Photography 2002–3*, Stedelijk Museum Amsterdam, 2003, cover
J.   Moyra Davey. *Speaker Receiver*, edited by Adam Szymczyk, Sternberg Press, 2010, back cover
K.   Michel Auder. *Stories, Myths, Ironies, and Other Songs: Conceived, Directed, Edited, and Produced by M. Auder*, edited by Adam Szymczyk and Quinn Latimer, 2014, Sternberg Press, back cover

Angie Keefer in conversation with Julia Born
Hudson, NY / Zurich, 19 March 2021

Angie Keefer Time is an important factor in your work, not least because you sometimes spend years developing a project. When you're first approached by someone who would like to work with you, how do you decide whether to commit, knowing how long the relationship may ultimately continue?

Julia Born My work is entirely built around conversation, so our ability to talk together is important. I am not only looking for consensus or agreement, but also friction or difference, because both are needed for a real dialogue to take place. If I feel there is someone critical on the other end, someone with questions and opinions – a sparring partner who challenges me as much as I challenge them – then I know there's a connection, so I do it.

Quite often that first conversation involves assessing expectations – capturing the brief for the project, yes, but sometimes reformulating it instead. That defining of the playground in which a collaboration will take place often leads to unexpected ways of approaching a project.

The way I work can be quite demanding or challenging in the sense that I need to be involved in the content on an editorial level, so it's necessary to be clear about that from the beginning. I dive into the texts and the image material at the outset to gain an understanding of intentions and methodologies, as well as references – all ways of thinking and acting. As a designer, I consider myself the first reader of a text and the first viewer of images. My principal questions are: "How would I like to read this text or see this material myself? What is intrinsic to these texts and images that requires a specific form?" Becoming familiar with the content and doing additional research goes hand-in-hand with articulating a visual language, including typefaces, for example, and developing ideas about materiality.

Making a book is an utterly laborious, sometimes exhausting process, which requires patience and stamina. I compare it to running a marathon – even when you think it's done, there's still so much left to do. When asked to make a book in the past, I have sometimes said no to books that I did not think were necessary or urgent to publish.

AK What is the longest time that you've spent on any single project?

JB The longest projects are the books in collaboration with Uta Eisenreich. The first one, *A NOT B*, took about three years to make. The second one, *AS IF*, is now in its final phase, and we have been working on it intermittently for about eight years. Uta is an artist based in Amsterdam – a photographer who also studied as a graphic designer. We met when we were students, and we realised that we shared many interests, particularly in how language is acquired and taught, such as in primary schoolbooks, which in turn shapes one's way of reading the world. We have a special way of working, because we have been in conversation for such a long time, and she continues producing work as a book develops. The narrative of the images and their sequencing are constructed over many iterations like a puzzle consisting of 5,000 pieces. Even during the final phase of the design and editing process, Uta is still generating new images, filling in gaps. This process sometimes reminds me of the way Samuel Beckett worked, finishing his theatre pieces on stage with the actors, making his last edits to the text after seeing it performed. The work with Uta is not a typical commission – it's disproportionately time-consuming – but the books are precisely distilled in the end, as if all our conversations were boiled down to one, comprehensively detailed take. That wouldn't work in every case; you can talk some material to death, whereas Uta's work gains even greater depth when refined repeatedly.

I sometimes engage in ongoing commissions for identities and cultural institutions like Casco, the Brücke-Museum and the Rijksakademie that last for many years. The most extensive has been *documenta* 14. It was a special experience, involving many artists, writers and curators as it took shape – from Adam Szymczyk's written proposal to two fully realised exhibitions in Athens and Kassel that required hundreds of people working together. The box of printed objects and the partial website that remain today cannot truly convey the significance and intensity of that project – the insights gained and the relationships formed through the working process.

AK You've done a lot of work with artists and art institutions. What importance do you think the structure of that field has for your work?

JB I was "raised", or, let's say, educated, at the Rietveld Academie in Amsterdam. As an institution or a school, the Rietveld is autonomous in spirit, encouraging students to develop a position, which helps to cultivate a special confidence. Back in the day, people would come to the graduation show and ask young students who had recently graduated to work on projects. One of my first projects was a book for Museum Boijmans van Beuningen in Rotterdam. I was a complete greenhorn! I didn't have a clue about making books, but that's how I entered this world. I find that people who work in this field are willing to engage and invest emotionally and intellectually in producing work on a high level. Quite often, too, the work does not need to answer directly to a sales objective, depending on how it is funded, and in this sense the sector is a distinctive niche.

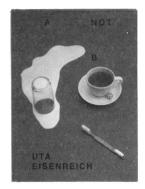 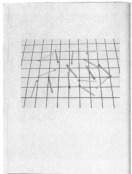   

L. Uta Eisenreich. *A NOT B*, Roma Publications, 2010, cover and spreads

Angie Keefer im Gespräch mit Julia Born
Hudson, NY / Zürich, 19. März 2021

Angie Keefer Ein wichtiger Faktor für deine Arbeit ist die Zeit, denn ein Projekt kann bei dir manchmal mehrere Jahre beanspruchen. Welche Rolle spielt diese potenziell lange Dauer bei deinen Entscheidungen, ob du dich auf eine vorgeschlagene Zusammenarbeit einlässt oder eher nicht?

Julia Born Meine Arbeit basiert vollumfänglich auf Gesprächen, deshalb ist es ausschlaggebend, ob ich mit jemandem gut diskutieren kann. Dabei geht es mir nicht nur um Konsens oder Einigung, sondern auch um Spannungen oder Meinungsverschiedenheiten, denn auch das ist für einen Dialog wichtig. Wenn ich den Eindruck habe, dass auf der anderen Seite eine kritische Person mit Fragen und Überzeugungen steht, die mich genauso herausfordert wie ich sie, dann gibt es eine Verbindung, und ich lasse mich darauf ein.

Beim ersten Gespräch geht es meist darum, die Erwartungen zu klären. Natürlich muss ich die Projektbeschreibung verstehen, aber manchmal formulieren wir sie dann auch um. Wir definieren gemeinsam das Spielfeld, auf dem die Zusammenarbeit stattfindet, und daraus ergeben sich oft unerwartete Herangehensweisen.

Meine Arbeitsweise kann ziemlich anspruchsvoll oder herausfordernd sein, weil es mir wichtig ist, auf der redaktionellen Ebene an den Inhalten mitarbeiten zu können. Das muss also zuerst geregelt werden. Dann tauche ich in die vorliegenden Texte und Bilder ein, um die Intentionen, Methodologien und Bezüge kennen zu lernen – die verschiedenen Denk- und Handelsweisen. Zur Rolle der Gestalterin gehört es meines Erachtens, dass sie die erste Leserin der Texte und erste Betrachterin der Bilder ist. Die Hauptfragen sind: «Wie würde ich selbst diesen Text gerne lesen oder dieses Material anschauen? Welche Eigenheiten der Texte und Bilder verlangen nach einer bestimmten Form?» Deshalb gehen das Kennenlernen der Inhalte und weiterführende Nachforschungen Hand in Hand mit der Entwicklung einer visuellen Sprache, zu der zum Beispiel die ausgewählten Schriften gehören, und mit der Ideenfindung bezüglich der Materialität des Buches.

Ein Buch zu machen ist ein arbeitsintensiver, manchmal ermüdender Prozess, der viel Geduld und Ausdauer verlangt. Ich vergleiche es mit einem Marathon – wenn du denkst, du hast es geschafft, taucht immer wieder eine neue Kurve auf. Wenn ich ein Buch nicht für notwendig oder dringlich halte, kann es vorkommen, dass ich eine Anfrage zur Zusammenarbeit ablehne.

AK Was ist die längste Zeit, die du jemals für ein Projekt aufgewendet hast?

JB Am längsten dauern die Bücher mit Uta Eisenreich. Für das erste, *A NOT B*, brauchten wir drei Jahre. Das zweite, *AS IF*, ist aktuell in der Endphase, und inklusive aller Unterbrüche haben wir ungefähr acht Jahre daran gearbeitet. Uta ist eine Künstlerin aus Amsterdam, die einst Fotografie in Dortmund und Grafikdesign in meiner Klasse studierte. Schon damals entdeckten wir viele gemeinsame Interessen. Dazu gehören der Erwerb und das Aneignen von Sprache, wie es in Grundschulbüchern vermittelt wird und wie es dann wieder die sprachliche Wahrnehmung der Welt beeinflusst. In den langen Jahren unserer Bekanntschaft haben wir uns eine spezielle Arbeitsweise angeeignet, bei der Uta fortlaufend Bilder produziert, während das Buch schon im Entstehen ist. Abfolge und Narrativ der Fotos werden in immer neuen Anläufen hergestellt, etwa so wie ein 5000-teiliges Puzzle. Sogar in der Endphase der Gestaltung und Redaktion macht Uta noch neue Bilder, um allfällige Lücken zu füllen. Es erinnert mich manchmal an die Arbeitsweise von Samuel Beckett, der seine Stücke auf der Bühne mit den Schauspielerinnen und Schauspielern fertigstellte, weil er sie anders nicht redigieren konnte. Uta und ich brauchen also unverhältnismässig viel Zeit, so dass es keine typische Auftragssituation ist, aber dafür sind die Bücher am Ende hochkonzentriert. Alle unsere Gespräche sind gewissermassen zu einer Aufnahme verdichtet. Die Methode lässt sich nicht auf alle Fälle übertragen, denn Dinge können auch totgeredet werden. Aber Utas Arbeit hat die Eigenheit, dass sie immer noch tiefgründiger wird, je mehr sie verfeinert wird.

Andere Arbeiten, die mich über mehrere Jahre beschäftigten, waren visuelle Identitäten für Kulturinstitutionen wie Casco in Utrecht, das Brücke-Museum Berlin oder die Rijksakademie Amsterdam. Am umfangreichsten war diesbezüglich die documenta 14, für die ich mit Laurenz Brunner kollaborierte. Das war eine besondere Erfahrung, denn von Anfang bis Ende – von Adam Szymczyks ausformulierter Bewerbung bis zu den grossen Ausstellungen in Kassel und Athen mit Hunderten von Mitarbeitenden – war für die Konzeption eine ganze Gruppe von Leuten zuständig: Künstlerinnen und Künstler, Autorinnen und Autoren, die kuratorische Leitung. Die Intensität und Bedeutung dieser Arbeit sowie die neuen Erkenntnisse und Beziehungen, die daraus hervorgingen, lassen sich aus der resultierenden Schachtel mit Druckbogen und dem heute noch zugänglichen Teil der Website kaum ersehen.

AK Du arbeitest sehr oft im Kunstbereich – sowohl für einzelne Beteiligte als auch für Institutionen. Welche Bedeutung

M. Casco, Office for Art, Design and Theory, Utrecht, visual identity, in collaboration with Laurenz Brunner, 2005–11
N. Brücke-Museum, Berlin, visual identity, in collaboration with Laurenz Brunner, since 2018
O. Rijksakademie voor beeldende kunsten, Amsterdam (poster for Open Studios 2019), visual identity, in collaboration with Linda van Deursen, since 2019

But I have worked outside of the arts at times. I did a project for the Dutch Royal Post Office, for example, who commissioned me to design a stamp. This was probably the largest edition of a work of mine – the stamp was printed in a run of around 300,000 – which was amazing to me, especially since this was considered a special edition and was only available for a limited time.

AK   You mentioned your experience at the Rietveld as a student, but you also taught there regularly for ten years from 2002 to 2012, at a time when a handful of young and internationally influential designers were teaching there, several coming from outside of the Netherlands, like yourself. Many of you became friends and collaborators. This opportunity for people from diverse backgrounds to meet as young designers and form a community within the academy seems to have been important, not only for you as individuals, but for the field of graphic design. How do you view the intersection of your roles as a designer and an educator and the importance of community, specifically with respect to institutions like art schools?

JB   I feel that teaching has been my second education. I didn't do a master's programme, but, through teaching, I've been able to continue exploring design and the field in a discursive way, by which I don't only mean theoretically; I see teaching as an extension of my practice. It forces me to think about the conditions of the profession, to question them, to renew or refresh my ideas about what I'm doing, and to keep up with current developments. I have often brought in projects or materials I'm actively dealing with and recommissioned my students to address questions that I don't already have answers to myself.

Of course, I have also met incredible people through this work – both students and teachers – and they have taught me at least as much as I taught them. The year I graduated from the Rietveld, Linda van Deursen became head of that department, and she brought several people in. Linda hired us for our very specific, personal ways of working, whether we were experienced teachers or not. We didn't have staff meetings and weren't organised around an explicit programme. Once a year we gathered at Linda's place for pancakes, but we didn't speak about school there – we just socialised. And we were indeed a happy community.

As a teacher, one learns a lot on a human level – how to read students as human beings, how to encourage them, when to protect them, or when to push them, if necessary – which is crucial within graphic design, since it's all about human relations and communication. The range of students is broad at the Rietveld, which is why I continue teaching there. It's a mix of people coming from all over the world, with different backgrounds and different stories, connected by a shared curiosity. Students are incredibly inventive and forced to improvise by necessity, especially at programmes with less funding.

AK   We began by talking about time and production. Now that we're on to money and education, it occurs to me that the span of your career, from the late 1990s until now, coincides with a period of profound technological change that has radically altered the possibilities for communication, lowering or eliminating barriers to entry like cost and certification. Anyone with a network connection and a smartphone can now design and publish online, instantly and cheaply distributing their creations to a global audience. As someone dedicated to a slower and in many ways more demanding production cycle, what is your perspective on the cultural transformations now under way? How do these changes affect the economies of your work?

JB   During my studies, my "interactive" teacher sat down with me in an Internet cafe and helped me sign up for a Yahoo account – my first e-mail address. When I started school, there were three desktop computers in the entire computer workshop. So, for my interactive classes, I sometimes did assignments without a computer, using my Yashica camera, dealing with *ideas* of interaction through analogue means. I learned to think digitally without having digital tools at hand. Acquiring software skills and accessing tools has become easier now, and therefore it is uninteresting to simply make something "well designed" or good looking. The question is why and how we do something – why and how do we articulate a certain position or perspective? Graphic designers exercise agency and must take responsibility as active forces in a process of shaping content, not just "decorating" surfaces.

I don't only support and produce slow design, though. I love ephemeral, superficial and formally beautiful things that may have a shorter lifespan or quicker expiration date. I think the issue comes down to what the content requires – what kind of treatment and time does one need to sit with something, to analyse it, to understand it, whether as a designer or an audience? We spoke about a book that requires eight years, but I often do that kind of slower work right alongside things that are produced much faster. I believe that the process of making something – the time invested into an object – remains perceptible when you hold that thing in your hands. The care and dedication that goes into editing content, regardless of whether it's analogue or digital, makes a thing valuable and relevant.

P.   *3 generaties koninginnen*, postage stamp, special edition (for registered mail), intaglio, offset printing. Commissioned by Koninklijke TNT Post, Den Haag, 2009

Q. Rietveld Berlin / Zurich, residency programme, in collaboration with Laurenz Brunner, since 2014. Left: Classroom with self-made furniture, Berlin, 2014. Middle: Welcome breakfast, Zurich, 2017. Right: Excursion to the Emma Kunz Centre, Würenlos, organised by Norm, 2017

haben die im Kunstbereich gängigen Organisations- und Arbeitsformen für deine eigene Herangehensweise?

JB Ich bin an der Rietveld Academie in Amsterdam «aufgewachsen», oder besser gesagt, ich wurde dort ausgebildet. Für eine Institution und besonders für eine Schule lässt die Rietveld ungewöhnlich viel geistige Autonomie zu. Sie ermutigt die Studierenden, eine eigene Position zu finden, und erleichtert es ihnen damit, ein berufliches Selbstvertrauen zu entwickeln. Zu meiner Zeit wurden die Diplomausstellungen von Verantwortlichen aus den Kulturinstitutionen besucht, die uns sofort Aufträge gaben. So kam es, dass eines meiner allerersten selbständigen Projekte ein Buch für das Museum Boijmans van Beuningen in Rotterdam war. Ich war noch komplett grün hinter den Ohren! Ich hatte keine Ahnung vom Büchermachen, aber so bin ich in die Kunstwelt eingetreten. Im Lauf der Jahre habe ich dort viele engagierte Leute getroffen, die emotional und intellektuell einen grossen Aufwand betreiben, um Werke auf hohem Niveau herzustellen. Ziemlich oft dienen sie auch nicht primär einem Verkaufszweck. So gesehen ist der Kunstsektor eine spezielle Nische.

Aber ich war gelegentlich auch ausserhalb der Kunst tätig. Beispielsweise gestaltete ich einmal eine Briefmarke für die niederländische Post. Das war die bis anhin höchste Auflage, die eine Arbeit von mir erzielte – etwa 300 000 Exemplare. Es war grossartig, umso mehr, als es sich um eine Sondermarke handelte, die nur während einer beschränkten Zeit erhältlich war.

AK Du hast an der Rietveld nicht nur studiert, du warst anschliessend auch während eines Jahrzehnts – von 2002 bis 2012 – regelmässig an der Lehre beteiligt. Ihr wart damals eine Handvoll junger und international einflussreicher Dozierender, viele aus dem Ausland, die sich anfreundeten und gelegentlich auch ausserhalb der Schule zusammenarbeiteten. Die Möglichkeit, sich in jungen Jahren mit Leuten aus ganz unterschiedlichen Kontexten zu einer Gemeinschaft zu entwickeln, scheint für euch als Individuen, aber auch für das Fachgebiet insgesamt wichtig gewesen zu sein. Welche Bedeutung hatte es für dich, dass du gleichzeitig Gestalterin und Dozentin warst? Und welche Rolle spielt die Gemeinschaftsbildung deines Erachtens für eine Institution wie die Kunsthochschule?

JB Das Unterrichten ist für mich wie eine zweite Ausbildung. Ich absolvierte zwar kein MA-Programm, aber als Dozentin konnte ich die gestalterische Praxis und das Berufsfeld in einer diskursiven Weise weiter erforschen. Ich bezeichne das aber nicht als Theorie, sondern ich sehe das Unterrichten als Fortsetzung meiner Praxis. Es zwingt mich, über die Bedingungen des Berufs nachzudenken und sie zu hinterfragen; meine Arbeit immer wieder neu zu betrachten und einzuschätzen; und über aktuelle Entwicklungen auf dem Laufenden zu bleiben. Im Unterricht behandelte ich oft Projekte oder Materialien, mit denen ich in der Praxis gerade beschäftigt war, und liess die Studierenden an Fragen arbeiten, auf die ich selbst noch keine Antwort gefunden hatte.

Natürlich lernte ich beim Unterrichten auch faszinierende Leute kennen – unter den Studierenden ebenso wie unter den Dozierenden. Von ihnen habe ich mindestens so viel gelernt wie sie von mir. In demselben Jahr, in dem ich mein Studium an der Rietveld abschloss, übernahm Linda von Deursen die Departementsleitung und stellte einige neue Dozierende ein. Sie wählte uns wegen unserer jeweiligen persönlichen Arbeitsweisen aus, nicht wegen allfälliger Lehrerfahrung. Es gab keine Teamsitzungen und kein ausdrücklich formuliertes Lehrprogramm. Einmal im Jahr trafen wir uns bei ihr zu Hause zu Pfannkuchen, aber nicht einmal da sprachen wir über die Schule, sondern es ging einfach darum, uns zu sehen. Und wir waren tatsächlich eine vertraute Gemeinschaft.

Dozierende müssen vor allem auch menschlich viel lernen: wie Studierende als Menschen zu sehen sind, wie sie ermutigt werden können und wann sie beschützt oder wenn nötig auch zu etwas gedrängt werden müssen. Solche Erfahrungen sind meines Erachtens gerade für die grafische Gestaltung hilfreich, denn in unserem Fach geht es ja primär um zwischenmenschliche Verhältnisse und um Kommunikation. Zudem ist an der Rietveld die Bandbreite der Studierenden besonders gross. Es kommen Menschen aus der ganzen Welt, die unterschiedliche Hintergründe und Geschichten mitbringen. Die Studierenden sind unglaublich erfinderisch, und oft ist die Improvisation existenziell, besonders in den schwächer finanzierten Programmen. Ich unterrichte auch heute noch sehr gerne dort.

AK Zu Beginn unseres Gesprächs ging es um Zeit und Produktion, und jetzt sind wir bei Geld und Ausbildung angekommen. In diesem Zusammenhang fällt mir auf, dass deine in den späten 1990er-Jahren einsetzende Laufbahn mit einem tiefgreifenden technologischen Wandel einherging, welcher die Möglichkeiten zur Kommunikation radikal

R. *Secret Instructions*, in collaboration with Alexandra Bachzetsis, Amsterdam, Zurich, Glarus, 2005–10
Left: 1 of 3 covers. Middle: Spread with scores. Right: Stage setup, Amsterdam (De Brakke Grond)

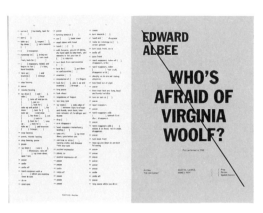

Adam [Szymczyk] once said that he is interested in stubborn repetition and errors that end up folded into the process, as opposed to wilfully formal innovations. Conflict, uncertainty and dissonance could be enemies of an "efficient" working method, but they allow for a layered perspective, or, even better, a multitude of perspectives, as opposed to just one, assured truth.

AK When speaking about your process earlier, you mentioned Samuel Beckett and alluded to his semi-improvisatory method of finishing a play by "editing" directly with the actors on stage. One of your long-time collaborators is a choreographer with whom you have worked closely on the production of theatrical pieces situated at a meeting point between graphic design, choreography and notation, which are translated into live, theatrical events. How has working in theatre and dance impacted your work, particularly the design of books?

JB That's an interesting link. The work I did together with Alexandra Bachzetsis started from a shared interest in language that we wanted to explore together. We're both interested in repetition as a device and a concept, and we both work with the construction of archetypes, often examining these ideas through different kinds of languages – verbal, visual and gestural. In *Secret Instructions*, we isolated the stage directions of six different playwrights, removing the rest of the content of the scripts, and then reformulated those directions as instructions for actors. This was a study of how implicit or explicit language might be and what impact it might have when interpreted as movement.

I referred to Beckett, because Beckett is an extreme example of someone who meticulously instructed his actors, down to the movement of their eyeballs 45° from left to right. He was hyper-precise and controlling. On the other hand there is Sarah Kane, who specified only a few stage directions in very general terms. Alexandra with her background in dance, performance and choreography was interested in the gestural aspects of language and how variations in the texts might translate into physical gestures.

Another piece we worked on, *This Side Up*, deals with a fundamental shortcoming of our language in the sense that when we say "up", "down", "left" or "right", the meaning we intend always depends on our own point of orientation. That led to a score that Alexandra eventually interpreted through movement, which we filmed by flipping the camera repeatedly so that it's no longer obvious to the viewer where gravity is – whether the dancer is on the floor, the wall, or the ceiling.

AK I was thinking about your own exhibition, *Title of the Show*, because exhibition design is also quite theatrical, and the metaphor of book design was especially strong in that instance. The experience of a visitor to the exhibition was of walking through an architectural translation of a book. Yet the publication you produced necessarily *followed* the installation of the exhibition, since the book consists entirely of installation photos, which contain within them all the "book" content – from the page numbers to the colophon and everything in between. So, a full circle is created via an architectural installation or theatrical production and a mated publication, with each of these elements anticipating and informing the others. The exhibition and the book become a physical dialogue, temporally and spatially interdependent.

JB Yes, definitely. The key to performance is its basis in time. You could say that the book is a more limited medium, but I am interested in interventions that open possibilities for interrupting or disrupting or changing the reading experience – how might narratives of beginning and ending be recomposed? There are common characteristics within performance and choreography and graphic design. As a designer, I construct narrative by orchestrating content – balancing voices, volumes and graphical gestures through stylistic, material and temporal means.

AK A sense of open-endedness and playfulness permeates your work, but you also make references to historical modernism and what has historically been conceived of as "Swiss design", which aspired to a certain clarity. You even quote directly from that canon at times, as in *Beauty and the Book*. Yet your work seems to undermine the heroic ideals and universalising aspirations of that era, inviting audiences to participate in a thought process that does not conclude – or was not concluded – with the production of the object. How do you think about ambiguity in your work? And how do you manage to achieve this ambiguity so consistently alongside the same graphic clarity that brings modernism to mind?

JB *Beauty and the Book* demonstrates how a myth – the idea of beauty – is constructed, and, at the same time, questioned and destroyed. I committed "crimes" against books, like dog-earing the pages and writing notes in the margins. I created these mistakes on purpose but also made them functional. I knew I couldn't make that book more beautiful than the ones featured within it, so I tried to formulate a meta-position, walking a thin line between beauty and ugliness, right and wrong, functionality, pure decoration, and

ausweitete. Einschränkungen durch hohe Kosten oder fehlende Berechtigungen wurden stark reduziert oder ganz eliminiert. Heute braucht man nur einen Internet-Zugang und ein Mobiltelefon, um gestalterisch und publizistisch tätig zu werden. Und die Arbeiten können unmittelbar nach Fertigstellung kostengünstig einem weltweiten Publikum zugänglich gemacht werden. Wie schätzt du diese kulturellen Umbrüche als eine Gestalterin ein, die langsamere und in mancher Hinsicht anspruchsvollere Produktionszyklen bevorzugt? Wie beeinflussen die Veränderungen die Wirtschaftlichkeit deiner Arbeit?

JB   Während des Studiums ging meine Dozentin für Interactive Design mit mir in ein Internet-Café und half mir, meine erste Yahoo-Adresse einzurichten. Am Anfang gab es an der Schule nur drei Rechner, weshalb wir in Interactive Design gezwungen waren, *Ideen* für Interaktivität auch mit analogen Mitteln auszuprobieren, z. B. mit meiner Yashica-Fotokamera. Wir lernten also digital denken, ohne wirklich digitale Werkzeuge zur Hand zu haben. Heute ist der Zugang zu Computer-Software und anderen Werkzeugen viel einfacher, und in der resultierenden Flut von Gestaltung haben frühere Kriterien wie «gut gemacht» oder «sieht gut aus» ihre Bedeutung verloren. Heute müssen wir uns vielmehr fragen, *weshalb* und *wie* wir etwas machen: Weshalb und wie nehmen wir eine bestimmte Perspektive ein? Gestalterinnen und Gestalter haben Autorschaft und müssen als aktive Kräfte Verantwortung bei der Gestaltung von Inhalten übernehmen, nicht nur Oberflächen «dekorieren».

Ich bin aber nicht nur eine Vertreterin von langsamer Gestaltung. Ich mag auch flüchtige, oberflächliche und formal schöne Sachen mit kürzerer Lebenszeit oder mit Verfallsdatum. Die zentrale Frage ist meines Erachtens, wonach ein Inhalt verlangt: Welche Art der Behandlung und wie viel Zeit sind nötig, um sich auf etwas einzulassen und um es zu analysieren und zu verstehen – egal ob als Gestalterin oder als Publikum. Wenn ich acht Jahre an einem Buch arbeite wie im Fall von Uta [Eisenreich], dann mache ich daneben auch ganze andere Dinge, die viel schneller fertig werden. Ich bin mir sicher, dass der Entstehungsprozess – und die investierte Zeit – wahrnehmbar bleiben, wenn man das fertige Objekt in den Händen hält. Dessen Wert und Bedeutung hängen primär davon ab, wie sorgfältig und engagiert der Inhalt erarbeitet wurde – egal ob analog oder digital.

Adam [Szymczyk] sagte einmal, er sei mehr an stureren Wiederholungen und den dabei entstehenden Fehlern interessiert als an bewussten formalen Innovationen. Zwar können Konflikte, Ungewissheit und Dissonanz «effiziente» Arbeitsprozesse behindern, aber sie ermöglichen auch mehrschichtige Betrachtungsweisen und im besten Fall sogar eine Vielfalt verschiedener Perspektiven anstelle einer einzigen, vermeintlich gesicherten Wahrheit.

AK   Als wir vorhin über deine Arbeitsweise sprachen, erwähntest du Samuel Becketts halbimprovisierte Methode, ein Stück auf der Bühne fertig zu redigieren. Du arbeitest seit langem eng mit einer Choreografin zusammen, mit der du auch Stücke an der Schnittstelle von Grafik, Choreografie und Notation produzierst, eines davon wurde sogar aufgeführt. Wie haben sich diese Erfahrungen mit Tanz und Theater auf deine Arbeit ausgewirkt, besonders auf die Buchgestaltung?

JB   Das ist eine spannende Frage. Meine Zusammenarbeit mit Alexandra Bachzetsis ging von einem gemeinsamen Interesse an sprachlichen Phänomenen aus. Wir nutzen beide verschiedene Arten von Sprachen – wörtliche, visuelle und gestische –, und wir interessieren uns für Ideen und Verfahren der Wiederholung sowie für die Konstruktion von Archetypen. Für *Secret Instructions* beispielsweise entfernten wir in Stücken von sechs Theaterautorinnen und -autoren sämtliche Dialoge, so dass nur die Regieanweisungen übrig blieben, die wir dann für die Darstellenden umformulierten. Wir untersuchten damit die expliziten und impliziten Bedeutungen von sprachlichen Anweisungen sowie die vielfältigen Möglichkeiten, sie in Bewegungen umzusetzen.

Beckett ist ein extremes Beispiel für penible Anweisungen an Schauspielerinnen und Schauspieler, bis hin zu einer 45°-Bewegung der Augäpfel von links nach rechts. Er war unglaublich präzis, aber auch besessen von Kontrolle. Einen Gegenpol dazu bildet Sarah Kane, die nur wenige Regieanweisungen in ganz allgemeinen Formulierungen verwendete. Alexandra mit ihrem Hintergrund in Tanz und Choreografie, interessierte sich auch für die gestischen Aspekte der Regieanweisungen und dafür, wie sprachliche Variationen in körperliche Gesten übertragen werden können.

In einem anderen Stück, *This Side Up*, beschäftigten wir uns mit einer grundlegenden Einschränkung unserer Sprache: Wenn wir zum Beispiel «oben», «unten», «links» oder «rechts» sagen, hängt die Bedeutung der Wörter von unserem jeweiligen Standpunkt ab. Wir thematisierten dies in einem Score, den Alexandra in Bewegungen umsetzte, und diese filmten wir unter mehrfacher Drehung der Kamera, so dass die Richtung der Schwerkraft am Ende nicht mehr offenkundig war. Es war unklar, ob sich die Tänzerin am Boden, an der Wand oder an der Decke bewegte.

AK   Auch Ausstellungsdesign kann manchmal theatral sein, und dazu fällt mir deine eigene Ausstellung *Title of the Show* ein. Sie benutzte Buchgestaltung als Metapher, denn sie führte das Publikum durch eine architektonische Umsetzung

 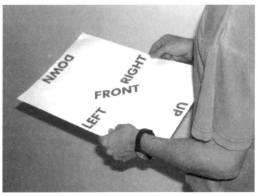

S.   *This Side Up*, in collaboration with Alexandra Bachzetsis, 2007. Left: *Performative Structures – New Existentialism Part 1*, Alte Fabrik Rapperswil, installation view © Gunnar Meier. Right: Poster, double-sided riso printing

uselessness. The rather unattractive cover with the giant ISBN number as large as the title was an intentional nod to the practices of libraries and archives of "killing" beauty by covering it up for purposes of protecting, preserving and indexing. But it simultaneously manifested a visual language typical for that time, which was associated with purity and elegance or perhaps a certain understatement, by removing a typographic hierarchy and levelling different types of information.

At first, my work may appear clear and simple visually, but that can be deceiving, because it never ends with clarity. I am "inviting the audience", as you say. A book should not impose a pre-fabricated view of the world, but rather offer a structure of possibilities for play. This opening of space for interpretation conflicts with the modernist ideals of objectivity and efficiency, and, in this way, ambiguity destabilises a seemingly solid structure, but it may happen quite subtly. I want to engage the reader. For me, it's important that you can look at something again and again. Maybe the second and third times, you see something else or you suddenly think, "Okay, I thought it was *this* way, but I could also read it *that* way."

I made a monograph with Wendelien van Oldenborgh, a Dutch artist and filmmaker, in which we featured ten of her films, as well as a lot of research materials, including scripts, dialogues, installations – polyphonic material. I had the idea to cut the pages horizontally so that whenever you flip through the book, you never see the same two pages or half-pages appear. The book is always different. This openness, demonstrated on a material level in the book, also represents her way of working. I often try to study someone at work, to understand their references or methodologies, and find ways to translate this into an object or layout – into a way of reading content. Content and form are inextricably connected and mutually dependent. To "design" means to organise content and therefore also to prioritise, to hierarchise – or de-hierarchise, for that matter. It means to select, process and filter content for a potentially wider audience, which makes the job a responsibility.

AK You've worked closely with several other visual artists for whom language is a primary subject and medium. I'm thinking of Moyra Davey and Shannon Ebner, for example. Their respective regard for language and the ways that they use language in their own work are so different, both from each other, but also from other artists you've spoken about.

JB I learned of Moyra [Davey]'s work when I was asked to produce a book, *Speaker Receiver*, which Adam [Szymczyk] edited. Her methods of narrating and editing fascinate me. Being both a writer, or a "speaker", and a reader, or a "receiver", describes my role as a graphic designer. One feature of the book was its blank spaces; I wanted the texts to pause whenever a work was mentioned and to display the image in question, before resuming with the text on the following page. I was interested in building a framework from the relationship between a blank page and silence – presence and absence.

With Shannon [Ebner], I made the book *A Public Character*, which involved a series of A's that were works which needed a place of display. Shannon sees and uses language as literal material – as substance and matter – something with a body and a physical presence. The letter A, according to her, manifests itself like a human body with legs. The relationship to typographic terminology that uses human metaphors – "type", "character", "family", "face" – is striking. In grammatical terms, A is an indefinite article, and we had many conversations about ambiguity and the potential in that which is not entirely clear or resolved. These discussions were inspiring for me, because I tend to strive for understanding – to create order and structure – but the project was a reason to consciously counteract that tendency and seek moments of irritation and indeterminacy instead. Our talks materialised in the decision to photograph a projection of her video *A Public Character* using a slow shutter speed, which resulted in double or multiple exposures, as opposed to using conventional stills, which would have lacked the sense of layered time that is so important within her work.

I am drawn to artists who engage with the everyday conditions of living as a metaphor for the human condition and its contradictions. Moyra and Shannon are very different artists with very different practices, but there is this connection.

AK It sounds like you're acknowledging and valuing doubt in an indeterminate process, rather than attempting to smooth that over for the sake of producing a superficially confident object. By foregrounding literal flexibility, as in the work with Wendelien [van Oldenborgh], or deliberately preserving irritation, as in the work with Shannon [Ebner], the process of adaptation between you and the artists, which renders the books, is potentially activated in the reader. As you put it, a reader might discover, "I thought it was *this* way, but I could also read it *that* way." That's doubt.

JB Making books, or maybe generally the activity of designing, is basically going through a list of a thousand questions, one after another, answering. I don't think I'm generally a doubter in the working process. Therefore, I work quite well with inconclusive people. But I have moments or periods of doubt and hesitation. In the moment

T. *Beauty and the Book, 60 years of The Most Beautiful Swiss Books*, Federal Office of Culture, Niggli Verlag, 2004, cover and spread

eines Buchs. Das Buch selbst entstand aber erst *nach* der Installation, denn es war gänzlich aus fotografischen Installationsansichten zusammengesetzt, die folglich sämtliche Komponenten des «Buchs» bereits in sich enthalten mussten: von den Seitenzahlen bis zum Impressum und alles dazwischen. So entstand ein Kreislauf zwischen einer architektonischen Installation – beziehungsweise einer Aufführung – und einer verwandten Publikation. Beide Arbeiten antizipierten und bereicherten sich gegenseitig, da sie in zeitlicher und räumlicher Verbindung in Dialog miteinander traten.

JB Meines Erachtens ist der Schlüssel zu jeder Perfomance die Verankerung in der Zeit. Im Vergleich dazu mag ein Buch als stärker eingeschränktes Medium erscheinen, aber mich reizen Interventionen, welche die Leseerfahrung unterbrechen, irritieren oder verändern. Wie können beispielsweise Erzählungen, die einen Anfang und ein Ende haben, neu zusammengesetzt werden? Es gibt also durchaus gewisse Eigenschaften, welche die Buchgestaltung mit der Choreografie und der Aufführung teilt. Als Gestalterin konstruiere ich Erzählungen, indem ich Inhalte orchestriere. Durch stilistische, materielle und zeitliche Mittel bringe ich Stimmen, Lautstärken und grafische Gesten in eine Balance.

AK Obwohl deine Arbeiten von Offenheit durchdrungen sind und oft etwas Spielerisches haben, beziehst du dich auch auf historische Tendenzen wie den Modernismus oder das *Swiss Design*, die eine starke Klarheit anstrebten. Manchmal zitierst du sogar direkt aus dem entsprechenden Kanon, wie zum Beispiel in *Beauty and the Book*. Dennoch scheinen deine Arbeiten die heroischen Ideale und universalistischen Ansprüche von Modernismus und *Swiss Design* zu unterminieren, denn durch die Offenheit lässt du die Leserschaft aktiv an einem Denkprozess teilhaben, der weit über die Produktion des Buchobjekts hinausreicht. Welche Rolle spielen dabei Verfahren der Ambiguität? Und wie arbeitest du mit Ambiguität, während du gleichzeitig eine fast modernistisch anmutende gestalterische Klarheit erreichst?

JB *Beauty and the Book* führte vor, wie ein Mythos – die Idee der Schönheit – konstruiert und gleichzeitig hinterfragt oder sogar zerstört werden kann. Ich beging bei der Gestaltung «Verbrechen» gegen das Buch, indem ich Eselsohren faltete und Notizen in die Randspalten schrieb. Dies waren absichtliche Fehler, aber sie sollten auch eine Funktion haben. Weil ich wusste, dass das Buch nicht schöner werden konnte als die darin porträtierten Bücher, versuchte ich eine Meta-Position zu formulieren. Dabei navigierte ich entlang einer feinen Linie zwischen Schönheit und Hässlichkeit; richtig und falsch; sowie zwischen Funktionalität, Dekoration und Nutzlosigkeit. Das wenig attraktive Cover mit der riesigen ISBN-Nummer beispielsweise, die gleich gross war wie der Titel, verwies auf die Praxis der Archive, welche die Schönheit oftmals überdecken müssen, um ein Buch zu schützen, zu konservieren oder in ihre Systeme einzuordnen. Gleichzeitig wurden dadurch typografische Hierarchien ausgeschaltet und verschiedenartige Informationen gleichbehandelt. Dies war eine damals geläufige visuelle Sprache, die für Schlichtheit, Eleganz und vielleicht auch für ein gewisses Understatement stand.

Meine Arbeit kann auf den ersten Blick klar und schlicht erscheinen, aber das täuscht manchmal. Du hast treffend gesagt, dass ich die Betrachtenden «teilhaben lasse», denn meines Erachtens sollte ein Buch keine vorfabrizierte Weltsicht aufdrängen, sondern die Buchstruktur sollte spielerische Möglichkeiten eröffnen. Es stimmt schon, dass solche Interpretationsspielräume im Widerspruch zu modernistischen Idealen der Objektivität und Effizienz stehen, und insofern kann die Ambiguität eine scheinbar solide Struktur destabilisieren, aber dies ist ein ziemlich subtiler Vorgang. Ich möchte die Leserinnen und Leser in erster Linie deshalb aktiv mit einbeziehen, weil es mir wichtig ist, dass man etwas wieder und wieder anschauen kann. Beim zweiten oder dritten Mal sieht man dann vielleicht plötzlich etwas Neues, oder man denkt, «Aha, ich dachte das war *so*, aber eigentlich ist es ja *anders*».

Für eine Monografie der niederländischen Künstlerin und Filmemacherin Wendelien van Oldenborgh, *Amateur*, die neben zehn Filmen auch vielstimmiges Material wie Drehbücher, Dialoge und Installationen zeigt, schnitten wir alle Seiten horizontal durch, so dass man beim Blättern nie dieselben zwei Seiten oder Halbseiten nebeneinander sieht. Das Buch ist jedes Mal anders. In diesem Fall kommt die Offenheit also auf der Ebene des Materials ins Spiel, was der Arbeitsweise von Wendelien entspricht. Ich versuche oft die Vorgehensweise der Leute zu studieren, um ihre Referenzen oder Methodologien zu verstehen und sie ins Buchobjekt oder in die Seitenlayouts zu übertragen – in die Art, wie der Inhalt gelesen wird. Inhalt und Form sind untrennbar verbunden und voneinander abhängig, denn «gestalten» heisst, Inhalte zu organisieren und dabei auch Prioritäten und Hierachien zu setzen – oder sie zu unterwandern. Inhalte müssen so ausgewählt, bearbeitet und gefiltert werden, dass sie potentiell ein breiteres Publikum erreichen können. Das ist die Verantwortung, die man übernimmt.

AK Du hast noch mit weiteren visuellen Künstlerinnen gearbeitet, für die Sprache ein wichtiges Thema und Medium ist, wie zum Beispiel Moyra Davey und Shannon Ebner. Beide haben jeweils ganz eigene Umgangsweisen mit Sprache, und sie unterscheiden sich auch von den anderen Künstlerinnen, über die wir schon gesprochen haben.

JB Moyra [Davey]s Arbeit lernte ich kennen, als ich von Adam [Szymczyk] für ihr Buch *Speaker Receiver* angefragt wurde. Ich finde ihre Art des Erzählens und Editierens sehr spannend, da sie sowohl als *Speaker* als auch als *Receiver* agiert. Als grafische Gestalterin sehe ich mich selbst in einem Zwischenbereich dieser beiden Rollen. Eine Besonderheit des Buches sind die vielen grossen Weissräume: Wenn im Text ein Werk erwähnt wurde, habe ich ein entsprechendes Bild eingefügt und den Text dann erst auf der nächsten Seite fortgesetzt. Mich hat interessiert, wie leere Seiten Stille evozieren und wie dies für den Aufbau einer Buchstruktur produktiv gemacht werden kann – als Wechsel von Präsenz und Absenz.

Mit Shannon [Ebner] machte ich das Buch *A Public Character*, das unter anderem eine Werkserie über den Buchstaben «A» zeigt. Shannon betrachtet und nutzt Sprache als eigentliches Material ihrer Arbeit – als eine richtige Substanz und Materie, die eine Gestalt und eine körperliche Präsenz aufweist. Der Buchstabe A manifestiert sich ihrer Ansicht nach ähnlich wie ein menschlicher Körper mit Beinen. Dies steht offenkundig in einem Bezug zu typografischen Fachbegriffen im Englischen, die menschliche Metaphern verwenden, wie z. B. «type» und «character» für Buchstaben, «face» für eine Schrift oder «family» für eine Gruppe von Schriftschnitten. Grammatikalisch ist «a» ein unbestimmter Artikel, und Shannon und ich führten lange Gespräche über Ambiguität und das Potenzial von Unklarheiten und von Ungelöstem. Diese Diskussionen waren für mich inspirierend, denn ich tendiere dazu, auf Verständnis hinzuarbeiten – auf die Herstellung von Ordnungen und

U. Shannon Ebner. *A Public Character*, ICA Miami, Roma Publications, 2016, cover and spreads

itself, I don't like to be in doubt, but later I realise that these uncertain states can be productive – they force me to think things through. I never leave anything unresolved. I eliminate the issues that come up in the process. But I do want to produce doubt *within* the work, in the reader or the viewer, as a way of engaging the viewer beyond that quick sense of "Oh, I get it", and that's it. This idea of irritation is the opposite of reassurance. I'm not trying to reassure the viewer.

AK You recently made a book with Elisabeth Wild, which is something that you were very eager to do. Coming back to my earlier question about how you know whether to engage – how did you know? What was it about Elisabeth's work that drew you to the prospect?

JB Eager. That's nicely put, because, after *documenta*, I said to Adam [Szymczyk], "If there is ever going to be a book about those collages, I want us to make that book", and he eventually invited me to do that. So, in a way, it was a dream come true. I had seen the film *Vivian's Garden* (2017), by Rosalind Nashashibi, which is about Vivian Suter and Elisabeth [Wild], who is Vivian's mother, in their home in Guatemala. But I find the question of exactly what it was about Elisabeth's work that drew me to it quite difficult to answer, because I simply fell in love. She's in Guatemala, in her house, she gets these magazines brought in, mostly from abroad, and from this material she creates a very rich image world in a loose and free-spirited way. The collages are quite small – they're more or less A4 paper size – but they're extremely powerful. And they're full of humour.

Working on this book was special, because Elisabeth passed away a few months before we began. I never met her in person, but I feel as though I know her in some way after making this book. Her presence was very strong in the stories and tales of the people who had known her, including Adam, Rosalind and, of course, her daughter Vivian, and these stories were the backdrop for the book. It reads like a piece of fabric, weaving together a life and work embedded in the places and languages in which she lived. We tried to make a book that would capture her with electric colour combinations or brutal material decisions like the cut on the fore edge. The images were carefully selected and sequenced by Adam and myself, and, for the first time ever, I placed all the work on the pages by eye, without any fixed coordinates, because there is no straight angle in the works themselves. Everything relies on intuition – just as in the not-exactly-square work on the cover. The scene of this woman focusing on her daily practice of producing mesmerising collages moves me. In retrospect, I see a parallel in her life to the circumstances in which this "lockdown book" was made: we were several people, each rather isolated somewhere in the world without much physical contact, diving together into the other-worldly spaces and dreams that were the realities of Elisabeth Wild.

Angie Keefer
Artist, writer, teacher and publisher,
Hudson/NY (USA)

Strukturen. Das Projekt bot mir Anlass, meine gewohnte Arbeitsweise bewusst in Frage zu stellen und nach Momenten der Irritation und Unentschiedenheit zu suchen. Unsere Gespräche führten unter anderem dazu, dass wir eine Projektion von Shannons Video *A Public Character* mit langer Belichtungszeit abfotografierten, was zu doppelten oder mehrfachen Belichtungen führte. Konventionellere Abbildungen hätten die mehrschichtigen Zeitebenen kaum zeigen können, die für Shannons Arbeit so wichtig sind.

Ich habe eine Vorliebe für Künstlerinnen und Künstler, die alltägliche Lebensumstände als Metaphern für die *condition humaine* und ihre Widersprüche behandeln. Dies verbindet Moyra und Shannon, obwohl sie sehr unterschiedliche Personen mit sehr unterschiedlicher Praxis sind.

AK Es scheint, dass du in einem Prozess Momente des Zweifels anerkennst und zu schätzen weisst, anstatt sie zugunsten eines scheinbar selbstbewussten Resultats zu übertünchen. Wenn du in deiner Arbeit mit Wendelien [van Oldenborgh] die Vieldeutigkeit hervorhebst, oder wenn du mit Shannon [Ebner] absichtlich Irritationsmomente beibehältst, dann wird dein Austausch mit der Künstlerin, aus dem die Bücher hervorgehen, potentiell auf die Leserinnen und Leser ausgeweitet. Wie du gesagt hast, kann dann etwas, das vermeintlich «*so* war», auch «*anders* gelesen werden». Das ist Zweifel.

JB Das Büchermachen oder vielleicht das Gestalten allgemein besteht meines Erachtens im Wesentlichen darin, eine Liste mit tausend Fragen eine nach der anderen abzuarbeiten. Ich würde sagen, dass ich generell keine Zweiflerin bin. Ich kann sogar ziemlich gut mit Leuten umgehen, denen es schwerfällt, Entscheidungen zu treffen. Aber natürlich erlebe ich auch Momente und Perioden des Zweifelns und Zögerns im Gestaltungsprozess. Das behagt mir im Augenblick gewöhnlich nicht, doch später merke ich dann oft, wie produktiv unsichere Zustände sein können, weil sie mich zwingen, etwas neu zu durchdenken. Ich lasse nie etwas ungelöst, sondern eliminiere die Schwierigkeiten, die sich im Verlauf einer Arbeit stellen. Aber für die Leserinnen und Leser lasse ich innerhalb eines Buches oder einer Arbeit gerne Momente des Zweifelns bestehen, damit sie nicht vorschnell denken, «das habe ich jetzt verstanden». Diese Art von Irritation ist das Gegenteil von Bestätigung. Ich versuche nicht, der Leserschaft Sicherheit zu geben.

AK Kürzlich hattest du Gelegenheit, ein Buch mit Arbeiten von Elisabeth Wild zu machen, auf das du dich sehr gefreut hattest. Ich möchte hier auf meine erste Frage nach deiner Entscheidungsfindung zurückkommen: Weshalb warst du so sicher, dass du das machen wolltest? Was hat dich so stark zu Elisabeths Arbeit hingezogen?

JB Mich darauf gefreut – das ist nett formuliert. In Wirklichkeit sagte ich nach der documenta zu Adam [Szymczyk], «wenn es jemals ein Buch über diese Collagen gibt, möchte ich das mit dir zusammen machen». Als er mich schliesslich dazu einlud, war es die Erfüllung eines Traums. Ich hatte Rosalind Nashashibis Film *Vivian's Garden* (2017) gesehen, für den sie Elisabeth [Wild] und ihre Tochter, Vivian Suter, in ihrem Haus in Guatemala besuchte. Aber was genau mich an Elisabeths Arbeit so anzog, ist nicht leicht zu beantworten, denn ich habe mich einfach verliebt. Sie lebt in diesem Haus in Guatemala, kriegt die Magazine – die meisten aus anderen Ländern – und schöpft daraus in assoziativer und freigeistiger Weise eine extrem reiche Bildwelt. Die Collagen sind eher klein – mehr oder weniger im A4-Format – aber äusserst kraftvoll. Und sie sind voller Humor.

Das Projekt war auch deshalb speziell, weil Elisabeth starb, bevor das Buch geplant wurde. Ich habe sie nie getroffen, aber seit der Arbeit an dem Buch meine ich, sie in gewisser Weise kennen gelernt zu haben. Sie wurde mir sehr präsent durch die vielen Geschichten und Anekdoten von Leuten, die sie kannten – darunter Adam, Rosalind und natürlich ihre Tochter Vivian. Wir nutzen diese Geschichten als Hintergrund des Buches, das sich nun wie ein Gewebe aus Leben und Werk lesen lässt. Es ist in die Orte und Sprachen eingebettet, in denen Elisabeth lebte, und wir versuchten sie auch durch elektrische Farbkombinationen und einen teilweise groben Umgang mit dem Material – wie den vorne bündig auf den Buchblock abgeschnittenen Festeinband – zu fassen. Adam und ich wählten die Bilder und die Abfolge, und zum allerersten Mal platzierte ich die Bilder mit blossem Auge auf den Buchseiten. Ich verwendete keine Koordinaten, weil es auch in Elisabeths Collagen keine exakten rechten Winkel gibt. Alles an dem Buch basiert auf Intuition, wie auch z. B. das nicht ganz rechteckige Stück Papier, das auf den Umschlag geklebt wurde. Wie diese Frau in ihrer täglichen Praxis diese hypnotisierenden Collagen produzierte, ist für mich schlichtweg bewegend. Im Rückblick erkenne ich zudem eine Parallele zwischen ihrem Leben und den Umständen, in denen dieses «Lockdown Buch» entstand: Alle Beteiligten befanden sich irgendwo auf der Welt in ziemlicher Isolation und hatten kaum physischen Kontakt, aber gemeinsam tauchten wir in die ausser-weltlichen Räume und Träume ein, die für Elisabeth Wild Realität waren.

Angie Keefer
Künstlerin, Autorin, Dozentin und Verlegerin,
Hudson/NY (USA)

Peter Knapp

Fotograf und Art Director

Photographe et directeur artistique   Fotografo e direttore artistico

Photographer and Art Director

Peter Knapp holding his personal research notebook – a collection of references and previous work
photographed by Diana Pfammatter, Zurich, 10 May 2021

Peter Knapp   Mit Panoramablick durchs Leben   von François Cheval

Peter Knapp ist ein Meister des Fotografierens und sein Beitrag zur angewandten Fotografie macht ihn seit den 1960er-Jahren zu einem bedeutenden Wegbereiter einer neuen Form der Modefotografie. Das alles steht ausser Frage, aber darauf reduzieren lässt er sich nicht.

Ist Peter Knapp tatsächlich ein Fotograf und sogar ein Schweizer Künstler? Er hat sich leidenschaftlich und regelmässig mit der Typografie und höchst sorgfältig mit dem Bildlayout einer Doppelseite auseinandergesetzt. Diese Storyboards haben es in die Museen geschafft und gelten in den Kunsthochschulen als Vorbilder. Ordnen, zuschneiden, verkürzen oder auflockern – all dies liegt seinen Plakaten, Einladungskarten und Filmen zugrunde.

Wie seine Vorgängerinnen und Vorgänger bewegte er sich in einem logischen Kontinuum (Müller-Brockmann, Miedinger, Ruder, Itten, Finsler, Frutiger) und bekannte sich dabei zu Einfachheit und Nüchternheit. Er nutzte die Schrift mit Eleganz, arrangierte die Bilder ohne den gesuchten Effekt und lehnte alles Dekorative ab. Nachdem er 1951 nach Paris gezogen war, führte er die Neue Sachlichkeit weiter, die er an seiner Schweizer Schule gelernt hatte, und erarbeitete eine ungekünstelte Darstellung des Objekts und eine Bildsprache, die sich zwischen Funktionalismus, Minimalismus und Universalismus situiert.

Es scheint also alles klar wie der blaue Himmel eines Morgens in den Bergen, heiter wie ein leerer Tempel ohne Verzierungen und erfüllt vom Verlangen nach Reinheit.

Aber man lebt nicht ohne Weiteres in Frankreich, in Paris, dem «24ème canton». Im Land der Autoritätsverweigerung greift Peter Knapp zur List. Er bricht mit der Tradition der radikal puristischen Ablehnung ungewöhnlicher Konstruktionen. Den Linien verleiht er eine subtile Sinnlichkeit und bringt die Kriterien von Design und Fotografie durcheinander. Immer wieder produziert er Zufälle. Er braucht und missbraucht und macht sich lustig über alles, was von der Kultur als gültig erachtet wird. Er erlaubt sich alles; in seinen Bildern scheinen die Frauen zu fliegen, indem sie ihren Körper befreien. Geometrie ist Verkrampfung. Der Sinn stiehlt sich aus dem Bild wie eine Onomatopoesie, die Wörter rennen über die Seiten und spielen mit den Illustrationen. Alles tauscht seine Bedeutung auf diesen befreiten Seiten.

Es ist schwierig, einfach zu bleiben, ohne Langeweile und ohne die Ausschweifungen der 1960er- und 1970er-Jahre in Frankreich. Ob für das Publikum oder für den Autor: Das Werk wirkt, weil es pures Leben ist und zur Freiheit einlädt. Peter Knapp gleicht denen, die es betrachten. Er wird nie satt davon, alles zu sehen. Als visueller Vielfrass, Zyklop mit Panoramablick, verfügt er über eine besondere Gabe. Ein grosszügiger Autodidakt? Bestimmt. Geschickt und diplomatisch? Gewiss. Aber diese Qualitäten könnten nicht zum Tragen kommen, würde er nicht über weitere seltene und kostbare Charakterzüge verfügen: die Ehrlichkeit und die Treue. Jede Seite, jedes Bild und jedes Buch sind eine Hommage an seine Freunde: In seinem grossen Repertoire, aus dem er schöpft, finden wir Zeichnungen von Steinlen, van Gogh, Gemälde von Tàpies, Césars Daumen oder Fotografien von Bruno Suter. Wie Jean Tinguely verarbeitet er Holz, Stahl und Kunststoff. Nicole de Lamargé wird zur Skulptur. Mit Courrèges erfindet er Le Corbusier neu. In Basel amüsiert er sich über Littmans Launen. Für sein Werk nimmt er oft die Hilfe von Poetinnen und Poeten in Anspruch, von Kreativen aller Art, von denen, die sich Neues ausdenken und sich nie mit der Gewohnheit begnügen: Hélène Lazareff, die ihm den Weg weist, oder Pierre Restany, dem er zuhört und den er versteht ... Die Liste ist unvollständig, es fehlen die gesehenen und kritisierten Filme, die auf Flügen verschlungenen Romane, die gesammelten Erinnerungen – und Christine ... Peter Knapp schafft Wahlverwandtschaften, aus denen sich die Gedankenwelt einer ganzen Generation erschliesst. Der Geist des Werks liegt in der unmittelbaren Zustimmung des Publikums.

Peter Knapp braucht mehr als ein Leben. Die Leben, die er bis jetzt geführt hat, schenkten ihm die Gelegenheit, starre Rahmen zu durchbrechen, und gaben Anlass, die eigene Meinung frei zu äussern. Sein Stil könnte so beschrieben werden, dass er den durchlebten Zeitabschnitten jeweils genau den passenden Ton in der entsprechenden Tonlage verlieh. Was die gesellschaftliche Bewegung von 1968 aufgebrochen hatte, setzte Peter Knapp mit seinen Filmen, in seinen Werken und seinen Plakaten um. Er war nicht der Einzige, aber er hat dazu beigetragen, die Fesseln von Sexismus und Rassismus zu lösen. Eine souveräne Freiheit äussert sich in jedem seiner Projekte, denn wir dürfen der Welt nicht gleichgültig gegenüberstehen und uns von der Selbstbezogenheit mitreissen lassen. Peter Knapp lässt die Jugend an seinen Überlegungen teilhaben, Generationen von Assistentinnen und Assistenten und Studierenden, die er der Normalität entrissen hat. Weitergeben ist eine Haltung. Zu den bereits genannten Werten kommt also noch das Weitergeben

dazu, das Vermitteln an junge Menschen, die dafür sorgen, die zeitlosen Praktiken weiterzuführen. Für ein Anwenden von Wort und Bild, das von Kunsthandwerk zeugt.

Der Schaffensmoment entsteht aus der eigenen Hand, die einen Strich zieht, auslöscht, wegkratzt und zerreisst, die zittert und alles in den Papierkorb wirft.

Das Paradox des Werks liegt im Ausdruck zwischen der persönlichen Geste und der Industrialisierung der Prozesse. Die Widersprüche der Moderne werden zu seinen eigenen. Seine Werke lassen sich vom Vulgären nicht beeindrucken und erschaffen Räume der Möglichkeiten. Licht und Dunkel, Serie und Einzelstück stehen sich zwar gegenüber, aber nichts schliesst sich gegenseitig aus. Wir stehen also tatsächlich vor einem zeitlosen Werk, wo sich Nachbildung und Original vermischen, wo sich der Überfluss zugunsten der Leere zurückzieht. Perspektiven und aufgebauschte Volumeneffekte verschwinden und stiften neuen Sinn.

Im Blau des Himmels betrachtet Peter Knapp den Abgrund. Er sieht die Hand seines Vaters, die Bäume, die Heuballen und die Weinstöcke. Für den Bergmenschen, der er geblieben ist, unterstreichen Schnee und Wälder, dass die Zeit der Illusion nicht die Zeit der Bilder ist. Der starke Willen eines Baums oder eines Kieselsteins, die Ästhetik des Unperfekten, dieses Nichts wirkt der allgegenwärtigen Eitelkeit entgegen.

Wenn er sich mit seinem Medium befasst, versucht Peter Knapp, die Dinge zu erhellen. Es ist eine Meditation, ein fröhliches, klarsichtiges Besinnen auf die Elemente der Wirklichkeit und ihre schicksalshafte Erscheinung: Das Überschreiten der Grenze zwischen Material und Verlangen, das Überwinden des unerträglichen Alltags durch die Bilder.

Peter Knapp   La vie avec une vue panoramique   par François Cheval

Si l'affiliation de Peter Knapp à la photographie, si son apport depuis les années 1960 à la photographie appliquée l'imposent comme un acteur majeur du changement de registre des images de mode, si tout cela est indiscutable, le réduire à ce domaine pose en revanche question.

Peter Knapp est-il véritablement photographe et même un artiste suisse ? Certes, il est celui qui a pratiqué avec ferveur et régularité la typographie et a agencé soigneusement ses images dans des doubles-pages. Ses chemins de fer ont rejoint les musées et sont donnés en exemple dans les écoles d'art. Dans ses affiches, sur ses cartons, au plus profond de ses ouvrages, au cœur de ses films, l'homme a ordonné, taillé, coupé, aéré. Comme ses prédécesseurs, dans un continuum logique (Müller-Brockmann, Miedinger, Ruder, Itten, Finsler, Frutiger), il a fait de la simplicité et de la sobriété une profession de foi. Il a su employer élégamment des caractères, disposer les images sans aucun effet, rejetant tout baroquisme. Dans la continuité de la Neue Sachlichkeit (nouvelle objectivité), ce membre de l'école suisse, émigré à Paris en 1951, a élaboré une représentation de l'objet et de l'image sans artifice, entre fonctionnalisme, minimalisme et universalisme.

Tout serait donc clair comme le ciel d'azur d'une matinée alpine, serein comme un temple vidé de toute ornementation et empreint d'une pureté virginale !

Mais on ne vit pas en France, à Paris, on n'habite pas le 24e canton sans risque. Contaminé par le mauvais esprit, dans ce pays de réfractaires à l'autorité, Peter Knapp ruse. Il lance sur les rails de la tradition de l'épure radicale des factures inhabituelles. En imposant à la ligne et à la diagonale une sensualité subtile, il affole et fait dérailler les critères du design et de la photographie. L'homme ne cesse de multiplier les accidents. Il use et abuse, il s'amuse de tout ce que la culture autorise. Tout lui est permis ; les filles s'envolent quand leur corps s'émancipe. La géométrie est spasme. Le sens s'échappe de l'image comme une onomatopée et les mots courent sur la page, jouent et se jouent des illustrations. Chacun échange ses significations dans des pages libres.

Il n'est pas si facile de rester simple sans ennui, et sans débordement, dans la France des années 1960–1970. Tant du côté du spectateur que de l'auteur, l'œuvre s'impose parce qu'elle n'est que vie et invite à la liberté. Peter Knapp ressemble à ceux qui le contemplent, il est ce gourmand jamais rassasié de tout voir, sans complexe. Il est doté, cet ogre visuel, ce cyclope à la vision panoramique, d'un don particulier. Autodidacte généreux ? Assurément. Agile et diplomate ? Certainement. Mais ces qualités ne s'exerceraient pas si l'homme n'était pas muni d'armes rares et précieuses, la sincérité et la fidélité. Qualités qu'il n'y a pour ainsi dire pas une seule image, pas une seule page, un seul livre, etc.,

qui ne soit un hommage aux amis : dans un grand fourre-tout, dans ce sac qu'il porte sur son dos, on trouve pêle-mêle des dessins de Steinlein, tout Van Gogh, des peintures de Tàpies, le pouce de César, des photographies de Bruno Suter, etc. Il bricole le bois, l'acier et le plastique à la manière de Tinguely. Il sculpte Nicole de Lamargé. Avec Courrèges, il réinvente Le Corbusier. A Bâle, il s'amuse des lubies de Littman, etc. L'œuvre ne serait pas sans la manière dont il demande constamment secours aux poètes, aux créateurs de toutes sortes, aux imaginatifs, à ceux qui ne s'accommodent jamais de l'habitude : à Hélène Lazareff qui lui indique le chemin, à Pierre Restany qu'il entend et comprend... Liste incomplète à laquelle il faut ajouter les films vus et critiqués, les romans dévorés dans les avions et les souvenirs accumulés, et Christine... Peter Knapp revendique des affinités électives qui dessinent le paysage mental d'une génération. La vertu de l'œuvre réside dans l'adhésion marquée d'emblée par les spectateurs.

Peter Knapp n'a pas assez de vies. Celles qu'il a vécues lui ont donné l'occasion de briser les cadres fixes et furent prétextes à la promotion de la parole libre. Et si l'on doit définir son style, disons qu'il a su donner le ton avec le timbre voulu aux temps qu'il a traversés. Ce que le mouvement social brisa en 1968, Peter Knapp le fit sur les écrans, dans ses ouvrages, en affiches. Il ne fut pas le seul, mais il participa à sa manière à arracher les baillons du sexisme, du racisme. Affirmation d'une liberté souveraine à chaque projet recommencé parce qu'on ne peut être indifférent au monde et laisser la vanité vous envahir. Peter Knapp prête son questionnement à la jeunesse, à des générations d'assistants et d'étudiants qu'il a ravies à la normalité. La transmission est une attitude. Ainsi aux vertus déjà relatées, ajoutons celle-ci, la transmission vers des jeunes gens en charge désormais de faire perdurer des pratiques hors d'âge. Pour un usage du mot et de l'image qui relève de l'artisanat.

Le moment créatif est le prolongement de la main, de la sienne propre, celle qui tire un trait, rature, gratte, déchire, tremble et jette à la corbeille.

Le paradoxe de l'œuvre réside dans l'articulation entre la revendication du geste et l'industrialisation des processus. Les contradictions de la modernité, il les fait siennes. Ses œuvres s'affichent étanches au vulgaire et créent des espaces du possible. Le lumineux et l'obscur se regardent en chiens de faïence, certes, le sériel et l'unique se côtoient, mais rien ne s'oppose. Nous voilà, preuves à l'appui, devant une œuvre dont le temps se confond pour inscrire le simulacre et le réel, quand la profusion se retire au profit de l'espace du vide. Voilà la signification de la disparition de la perspective et l'horreur affichée des effets de volume.

Dans le bleu du ciel, c'est l'abîme que Peter Knapp contemple. Il y voit la main de son père, les arbres, les bottes de foin, les ceps de vigne. Pour le montagnard qu'il est resté, la neige et les forêts soulignent que le temps de l'illusion n'est pas le temps de l'image. La volonté tenace d'un arbre, d'un galet, c'est dans cette esthétique de l'imperfection, dans ce rien, que la résistance à la vanité qui nous entoure fait œuvre.

En se penchant sur le médium, Peter Knapp a cherché à élucider ses enjeux. Il faut y voir une œuvre de méditation, un recueillement joyeux et lucide sur les éléments du réel et leur fatale apparence : le franchissement de la frontière entre la matière brute et le désir, le quotidien insoutenable et son nécessaire dépassement par la révélation de l'image.

Peter Knapp La vita con una vista panoramica di François Cheval

Se il nome di Peter Knapp è indissolubilmente legato alla fotografia e se il suo apporto alla fotografia applicata dagli anni Sessanta in poi ha imposto un cambiamento di registro nelle immagini di moda, se tutto ciò è indiscutibile, confinarlo in questo ambito solleva però un dubbio.

Ma Peter Knapp è davvero un fotografo e anche un artista svizzero? Certo, ha praticato con fervore e regolarità la tipografia e disposto con cura su pagine doppie le sue immagini. Le suoi menabò sono esposti nei musei e citati come esempio nelle scuole d'arte. Sui suoi manifesti, sui suoi cartoni, nel profondo delle sue opere, nel cuore dei suoi film, Peter Knapp ha ordinato, sfoltito, tagliato, arieggiato. In continuità logica con i suoi predecessori (Müller-Brockmann, Miedinger, Ruder, Itten, Finsler, Frutiger), ha fatto della semplicità e della sobrietà una professione di fede. Ha saputo impiegare elegantemente i caratteri e disporre le immagini senza creare alcun effetto, rifuggendo da ogni barocchismo. In continuità con la Nuova oggettività, questo esponente della scuola svizzera emigrato a Parigi (1951) ha elaborato una rappresentazione scabra dell'oggetto e dell'immagine, tra funzionalismo, minimalismo e universalismo.

Tutto sarebbe dunque chiaro come il cielo azzurro in una mattinata alpina, sereno come un tempio spogliato di ogni ornamento e permeato di purezza virginale.

Ma non si vive in Francia e tantomeno a Parigi, la città immortalata da Peter Knapp come ventiquattresimo Cantone svizzero, senza correre rischi. Contagiato dallo spirito maligno di questo Paese di refrattari all'autorità, l'artista gioca d'astuzia. E rompe con la tradizione dell'epurazione radicale di ogni forma inusitata. Imponendo alla linea e alla diagonale una sensualità sottile, sconvolge e fa deragliare i criteri del design e della fotografia. E moltiplica senza sosta gli incidenti. Usa e abusa, gioca con tutto ciò che la cultura autorizza. Tutto gli è permesso; le ragazze prendono il volo quando i loro corpi si emancipano. La geometria è spasmo. Il senso sfugge all'immagine come un'onomatopea e le parole scorrono sulla pagina giocando e burlandosi delle illustrazioni. Ognuno scambia i propri significati su pagine libere.

Non è così facile restare semplici senza noia e senza eccessi nella Francia degli anni tra il 1960 e il 1970. Tanto dal punto di vista dello spettatore che da quello dell'autore, l'opera s'impone perché non è altro che vita e invita alla libertà. Peter Knapp assomiglia a quelli che lo contemplano, è un goloso mai sazio di vedere tutto, senza complessi. Orco visuale e ciclope dallo sguardo giroscopico, ha un dono particolare. Autodidatta generoso? Sicuramente. Agile e diplomatico? Certamente. Ma queste qualità non gli servirebbero a nulla se non fosse dotato di due armi rare e preziose: la sincerità e la fedeltà. Non c'è una sola immagine, una sola pagina, un solo libro di lui, che non sia anche un omaggio agli amici. Nel bagaglio stracolmo che porta con sé si trova di tutto: disegni di Steinlein, tutto van Gogh, dipinti di Tàpies, il pollice di César, fotografie di Bruno Suter ecc. Lavora il legno, l'acciaio e la plastica alla maniera di Tinguely. Scolpisce Nicole de Lamargé. Con Courrèges, reinventa Le Corbusier. A Basilea, si prende gioco dei ghiribizzi di Littman. La sua opera non esisterebbe senza quel suo modo di chiedere costantemente aiuto ai poeti, ai creativi di ogni tipo, agli immaginifici, a coloro che non si accontentano mai dell'usuale: a Hélène Lazareff, che gli mostra il cammino, a Pierre Restany, che ascolta e comprende... Un elenco incompleto cui vanno aggiunti i film che ha visto e criticato, i romanzi divorati sugli aerei e i ricordi accumulati, e Christine... Peter Knapp rivendica affinità elettive che riflettono il mondo interiore di una generazione. La virtù dell'opera risiede nell'immediata e convinta adesione degli spettatori.

Peter Knapp non ha abbastanza vite. Quelle che ha vissuto gli hanno dato l'occasione di rompere gli schemi e sono state pretesto per promuovere la parola libera. E se dobbiamo definire il suo stile, diciamo che ha saputo dare il tono con il timbro richiesto nei tempi che ha attraversato. La rivoluzione del Sessantotto, Peter Knapp l'ha fatta sullo schermo, nelle sue opere, sui suoi manifesti. Non è stato il solo, ma a modo suo ha contribuito a strappare i bavagli del sessismo e del razzismo. Affermazione di una libertà sovrana ad ogni progetto ricominciato, perché non si può essere indifferenti al mondo e lasciarsi invadere dalla vanità. Peter Knapp presta i suoi interrogativi alla gioventù, a generazioni di assistenti e studenti che ha sottratto alla normalità. La trasmissione è un atteggiamento. Così alle virtù già enumerate possiamo aggiungere anche questa: l'ispirazione della gioventù a far perdurare pratiche fuori tempo. Per un uso della parola e dell'immagine che affonda le sue radici nell'artigianato.

Il momento creativo è il prolungamento della propria mano, di quella che tira una riga, barra, raschia, straccia, trema e butta nel cestino.

Il paradosso della sua opera risiede nella compresenza della rivendicazione del gesto e dell'industrializzazione dei processi. In sintonia con i tempi, fa sue le contraddizioni della modernità. Impermeabili ad ogni volgarità, le sue opere creano spazi del possibile. Certo, la luminosità e l'oscurità si guardano in cagnesco, il seriale coesiste con l'unico, e con questo? Eccoci dunque, prove alla mano, di fronte a un'opera il cui tempo si confonde per iscrivere il simulacro e il reale, quando la profusione si ritira a vantaggio dello spazio del vuoto. Ecco il significato della scomparsa della prospettiva e dell'orrore ostentato degli effetti di volume.

Nell'azzurro del cielo, Peter Knapp contempla l'abisso. Ci vede la mano di suo padre, gli alberi, le balle di fieno, le vigne. Per il montanaro che è rimasto, la neve e i boschi sottolineano che il tempo dell'illusione non è il tempo dell'immagine. La volontà tenace di un albero o di un ciottolo: è in quest'estetica dell'imperfezione, in questo nulla, che agisce la resistenza alla vanità che ci circonda.

Peter Knapp ha cercato di far passare i suoi messaggi servendosi sapientemente degli strumenti impiegati. La sua opera va intesa come un'opera di meditazione, un raccoglimento gioioso e lucido sugli elementi del reale e la loro fatale apparenza: l'attraversamento del confine tra la materia grezza e il desiderio, il quotidiano insostenibile e il suo necessario superamento attraverso la rivelazione dell'immagine.

Peter Knapp A Life with a Panoramic View   by François Cheval

Peter Knapp's dedication to photography in general and his contribution to applied photography in particular since the 1960s mark him out as a key figure in the transformation of fashion imagery. Yet surely, he is much more than this.

In fact, we might ask: is Peter Knapp really a photographer; indeed, is he even a Swiss artist? He has undoubtedly been an enthusiastic and regular practitioner of typography, meticulously arranging his images across double-page spreads. His flat-plans have found their way into museums and are held up as examples in art schools. In everything from posters and works on card to films, he has organised, trimmed, cut, and freed up space. Like his predecessors in a logical continuum that spans Müller-Brockmann, Miedinger, Ruder, Itten, Finsler and Frutiger, he has made simplicity and sobriety an article of faith. He has deployed typefaces with elegance and arranged images without effects, abjuring all Baroque flourishes. Emigrating to Paris in 1951, he pursued the tradition of Neue Sachlichkeit (New Objectivity) that he learnt at his school in Switzerland, devising a way of representing objects that eschews artifice and an imagery that combines functionalism, minimalism and universalism.

So it seems everything is as clear as the blue sky of an Alpine morning, serene as a temple devoid of ornament and imbued with virginal purity!

But it's not so straightforward, living in Paris, France, the "24th canton". In a country that rejects authority, Peter Knapp resorts to cunning. He breaks with the radically purist tradition of repudiating unconventional constructions. Imposing a subtle sensuality on lines and diagonals, he disrupts the criteria of design and photography. He is a constant source of chance events. He uses, misuses and amuses himself with everything that culture values. He accepts no limitations: women take flight as their bodies break free. Geometry is paralysis. Meaning escapes from the image like an onomatopoeia while words run across the pages, playing with the illustrations, exchanging meanings as they relish their freedom.

It isn't easy to keep things simple and avoid boredom or excess in 1960s and 1970s France. For audience and author alike, the work functions because it is pure life and an invitation to liberty. Peter Knapp views as others do; he never tires of seeing everything. This visual ogre, this Cyclops with panoramic vision, has a particular gift. A generous autodidact? Unquestionably. Skilful and diplomatic? Certainly. But those qualities would mean nothing if the man himself were not endowed with the rare and precious traits of sincerity and fidelity. There is, seemingly, not a single image, page or book that is not a homage to his friends: amidst his vast repertoire, we find drawings by Steinlein and van Gogh, paintings by Tàpies, César's "Thumb" and photographs by Bruno Suter. He tinkers with wood, steel and plastic in the manner of Tinguely. He sculpts Nicole de Lamargé. With Courrèges, he reinvents Le Corbusier. In Basel, he entertains himself with Littman's whims. He frequently draws on poets, creators of all kinds, people who have imagination and are never content with the familiar: Hélène Lazareff, who shows him the way; Pierre Restany, whom he listens to and understands... Not to mention the films he has seen and critiqued, the novels devoured on planes, the memories accumulated, and Christine... Peter Knapp creates elective affinities that map out the mental landscape of an entire generation. His work's spirit resides in the instant approval of his audience.

Peter Knapp needs more than one life. The ones that he has lived so far have given him the chance to break free from rigid frameworks and state his opinions freely. In terms of style, he has found the perfect tone or timbre for each period through which he has lived. The social movement of 1968 forced open the gates and Peter Knapp transposed it all to the screen, his works and his posters. He was not alone, but he helped to shake off the bonds of sexism and racism. Each project is a renewed affirmation of sovereign liberty, because we cannot be indifferent to the world and retreat into self-absorption. Peter Knapp enables young people – the generations of assistants and students that he has torn away from normality – to participate in his investigations. And then there is his urge to share, to impart knowledge to young people who will be responsible for enabling ageless practices to endure. For a use of the word and the image that exudes craftsmanship.

The creative moment is the extension of his own hand, drawing a line, erasing, scratching out, tearing up, shaking and throwing into the wastepaper basket.

The work's paradox lies in the articulation between the personal gesture and the industrialisation of processes. Knapp makes modernity's contradictions his own. His works are impervious to vulgarity and create spaces for the possible. Light and dark come face to face; the serial appears opposite

the unique – yet neither excludes the other. What we have here, then, is a timeless body of work in which replica and original blur into one another, and excess gives way to emptiness. Perspectives and overblown effects of volume disappear, and new meaning emerges.

Amidst the blue of the sky, Peter Knapp is contemplating the abyss. In it, he sees his father's hand, the trees, the haystacks and the vines. For a man who has remained true to the mountains, snow and forests underscore that the time of illusion is not the time of the image. The tenacious will of a tree or a pebble, the aesthetic of imperfection, the nothingness, all resists ubiquitous vanity.

In his devotion to his medium, Peter Knapp has sought to shed light. His is a meditation, a joyous and lucid reflection on the elements of the real and their fateful appearance: a crossing of the boundary between matter and desire; an overcoming of the unbearably quotidian through imagery.

François Cheval
Künstlerischer Leiter und Ausstellungskurator, Chalon-sur-Saône (FR)
Directeur artistique et commissaire d'exposition, Chalon-sur-Saône (FR)
Direttore artistico e curatore di mostre, Chalon-sur-Saône (FR)
Artistic director and exhibition curator, Chalon-sur-Saône (FR)

Peter Knapp

1931	Born in Bäretswil	1960	First fashion photographs
1937-47	Primary and secondary school in Zurich	1964	Uses a Paillard-Bolex 16mm camera to capture movement. Assists Peter Foldes and Chris Marker
1945	Discovers photography		
1947-50	Student in the Graphic Arts Department of the Zurich School of Arts and Crafts, course inspired by the Bauhaus. Takes photography lessons	1965	Embarks on a 25-year collaboration as a fashion photographer with André Courrèges and Emanuel Ungaro, with whom he will remain very close
1948-50	Turns to painting and works in the studios of Monticelli and Otto Bachmann	1965-68	Directs 42 *Dim, Dam, Dom* films for French television, Paris, produced by Daisy de Galard
March 1951	Arrives in Paris. Studies for several months in the Architecture Department of the School of Fine Arts, Paris, where he meets César and Pierre Dmitrienko, who will remain his friends. Student at the Académie Julian	1966	Leaves *Elle* when Hélène Lazareff departs and becomes a freelance photographer for *Vogue*, *Stern* and *The Sunday Times*
1952-59	Freelance painter and graphic designer in Paris, Brussels and New York	1966	Gives up painting to devote himself entirely to photography
1953	Graphic designer in the studio of Paul Marquet. Redesigns the logos of NRF and Gallimard		Diversifies his activities, working as a set designer for the theatre on plays by Max Frisch and Eugène Ionesco
1953-55	Recruited by Hélène Lazareff, who is responsible for the visual identity of *Nouveau Femina*	1966	First medal from the Art Directors Club International; sixteen more will follow
	Works with literary director Roger Nimier, photographer Fouli Elia and graphic designer Antoine Kieffer	1967	Joins Oliviero Toscani to establish *Vogue* in Italy
1955	First photographic works	1967-92	Art director of André Sauret publications. The "Livres de la Santé" collection cements his collaboration with Raymond Lévy for the publishers Rencontre in Lausanne.
1955-59	Recruited by the director Jean Adnet and becomes art director at Galeries Lafayette. Oversees the design of posters and advertisements		
	Works with graphic designer Jean Widmer, designer Slavik and William Klein, on photography	1969	First international Nikon award
		1970	*Osaka*: artist's book devoted to the Expo '70 world's fair with Bruno Suter for the publisher Hermann
1959	Travels to New York as assistant to Jean Tinguely. The works of Robert Rauschenberg and Barnett Newman encourage him to produce large-format paintings.		
		1970	Art director of *Zeit Magazin* in Hamburg
	Develops a personal oeuvre that draws on the lyrical abstraction movement	1974-77	Returns to the magazine *Elle* to take up the position of art director
1959-66	Works as a photographer for *Elle* before accepting the post of art director offered to him by Hélène Lazareff		Works with the photographers Hans Feurer, Lothar Schmid and others
		1975	His personal work on the themes of the infinite, the sky and space brings him into the Sky Art movement.
	Takes charge of graphic identity and modernises the magazine. Inspired by Alexey Brodovitch and Henry Wolf, he pursues the democratisation of fashion and its new visual language.	1976-78	Major collaboration with Thierry Mugler and Claude Montana on series of photographs featuring Surrealist scenarios
		1981	His interest in contemporary art leads him to create the layout for a collection of works entitled "Contemporains" published by the Centre Georges Pompidou.
	Hires leading photographers (Robert Frank, Sarah Moon, Frank Horvat, Jeanloup Sieff, etc.) and illustrators (Jean-Michel Folon, Roland Topor, Roman Cieślewicz and others)		
		1983	Art director of Décoration Internationale

1983–96	Professor of image design and photography at ESAG (École supérieure d'Art Graphique, the former Académie Julian) at the invitation of his friend Roman Cieślewicz
1988	Art director of *Fortune*
1989	Best Art Book award for *Lumières de Chartres*, illustrated with photographs by Eustachy Kossakowski
1991	Best Art Book award for *Giacometti*, illustrated with his own photographs
2001	Produces seven portraits of graphic designers for the congress of the Alliance Graphique Internationale at the French National Library
2003	Makes *Ces appareils qui nous ont vus*, a series of three films on the history of photography, for TV 5
2005	Makes drawn films for *Lot et ses filles* (text by Michel Balmont)
2006	Makes a documentary entitled *Van Gogh, derniers jours à Auvers-sur-Oise* Peter Knapp is a member of Rencontres de Lurs and AGI (Alliance Graphique Internationale) and lecturer at Sciences-Po.
2021	Curates the exhibition *The Giacometti: A Family of Creators*, Fondation Maeght, Saint-Paul de Vence

Selected exhibitions

1958	Galerie Saint Germain, Paris (FR)
1966	*Schweizerfahnen*, Galerie Palette, Zurich
1975	*Il fait beau*, Galerie Denise René, Paris (FR)
1978	Rencontres Internationales de la Photographie d'Arles (FR)
1986	*Peter Knapp retrospective*, Paris Art Center, Paris (FR)
1988	*Aeroflag*, Galerie Littmann, Basel
1988	*Corpoflag*, Photokina, Cologne (DE)
1990	*Grand maquillage*, Art Expo, Tokyo (JP)
1993	*Photos d'elles. Temps de pose: 1950–1990*, Centre de la Photographie, Geneva
2000	*Le siècle du corps: Photographie 1900–2000*, Musée de l'Elysée, Lausanne
2001	*Les années pop*, Centre Pompidou, Paris (FR)
2008	*Peter Knapp ou la passion des images*, Maison européenne de la Photographie, Paris (FR)
2008	*Peter Knapp, directeur artistique*, Galerie Anatome, Paris (FR)
2009	*The Last Waltz*, Musée Nicéphore Niépce, Chalon-sur-Saône (FR)
2009	*Sur le fil du film*, Théâtre de la photographie et de l'image, Nice (FR)
2014	*Peter Knapp. Elles, 101 regards sur les femmes*, Musée des Suisses dans le Monde, Geneva
2017	*Peter Knapp, illustrateur – Dessins 1952–2016* Musée Tomi Ungerer, Strasbourg (FR)
2018	*Dancing in the Street. Peter Knapp et la mode 1960–1970*, Cité de la Mode et du Design, Paris
2000	*Homme de paille*, Musée Nicéphore Niépce, Chalon-sur-Sâone (FR)
2022	Peter Knapp (solo show), Fotostiftung Winterthur

A, B

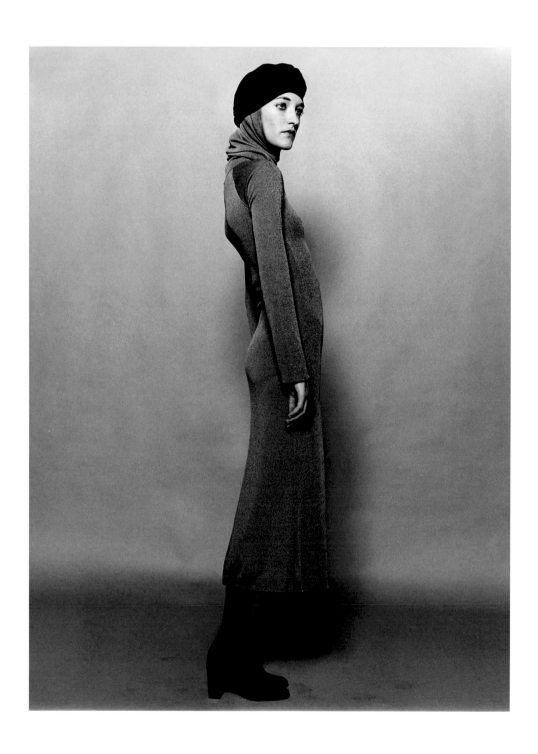

E, F

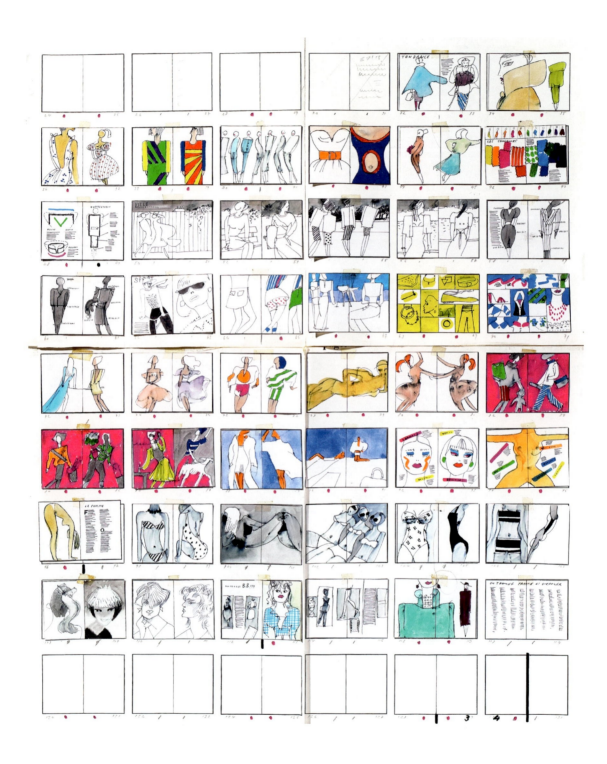

I, J

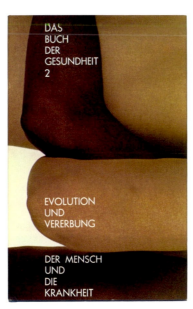

L, M, N

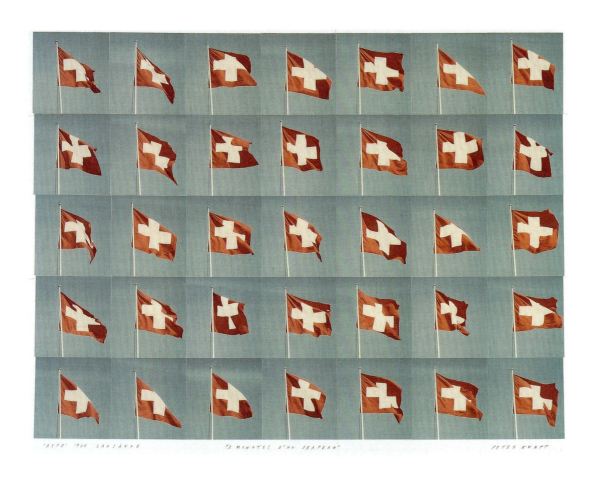

O, P

A. Peter Knapp (photography and art direction) for *Elle*, Paris, 1962 © Archive Peter Knapp
B. Peter Knapp, Nicole de Lamargé, "Avant-Après", *Elle*, March 1966 © Archive Peter Knapp
C. Peter Knapp, Loulou de la Falaise in Loulou de la Falaise, Paris, 1967 © Archive Peter Knapp
D. Peter Knapp, Thierry Mugler collection "Spirale futuriste", autumn-winter 1979–80, Paris, 1979 © Archive Peter Knapp
E. Peter Knapp, Rita Scherrer, *Vogue*, Paris, 1967 © Archive Peter Knapp
F. Peter Knapp, *Hommage à Albers*, 1989 © Archive Peter Knapp
G. Peter Knapp, Fashion for *Stern*, 1979 © Archive Peter Knapp
H. Peter Knapp, advertisement for Dim, coloured tights, Paris, ca. 1968 © Sammlung Fotostiftung Schweiz
I. Peter Knapp, flatplan, n.d. © Archive Peter Knapp
J. Peter Knapp, Louise Despointes, "Pastels are prettier", *British Vogue*, June 1972 © Archive Peter Knapp
K. Peter Knapp, Christiana Steidten in Daniel Hechter, *Marie Claire*, February 1972 © Archive Peter Knapp
L. Peter Knapp, Pierre Cardin, collection autumn-winter, 1968 © Archive Peter Knapp
M. Peter Knapp (art direction and graphic design), *Das Buch der Gesundheit 15. Bakterien, Viren, Strahlung*, Monte Carlo: André Sauret, 1969 © Museum für Gestaltung Zürich, Graphics Collection, ZHdK
N. Peter Knapp (art direction and graphic design), *Das Buch der Gesundheit 2. Evolution und Vererbung. Der Mensch und die Krankheit*, Monte Carlo: André Sauret, 1976 © Museum für Gestaltung Zürich, Graphics Collection, ZHdK
O. Peter Knapp, *Drei Minuten einer Flagge*, 1964
P. Peter Knapp (photography and art direction), Les minijupes, *Elle*, May 1966 © Archive Peter Knapp

Tatyana Franck en conversation avec Peter Knapp
Lausanne, 18 mars 2021

Tatyana Franck Peter Knapp, vous êtes photographe, cinéaste, graphiste, peintre, dessinateur, directeur artistique, enseignant, vous êtes un véritable faiseur d'images. Aujourd'hui, à 90 ans, vous avez encore cet enthousiasme extraordinaire et ce regard vif. Qu'est-ce qui vous motive? Quel est votre moteur dans la vie?

Peter Knapp Ce qui me motive, c'est traduire des idées en images. Essayer de transcrire ce que je pense, ce que j'invente, ce que j'ai envie de raconter en images. Je suis admiratif de Charlie Chaplin et de Federico Fellini, qui réussissent à être visuellement aussi narratifs. Moi, je suis tour à tour cinéaste ou photographe. C'est le concept qui détermine l'outil que j'utilise.

Quand j'étais encore étudiant, j'avais acheté un livre sur Léonard de Vinci, sur la méthode de la peinture. Le livre m'avait coûté cher et c'était une déception au final parce qu'il traitait principalement de la chimie et de la fabrication de la peinture. Comme la peinture était très chère à l'époque, je me souviens que le livre proposait de favoriser les fonds noirs parce que le noir était plus abordable. Mais une phrase m'a marqué et compte encore aujourd'hui: une idée n'est rien si elle n'est pas saisie dans un dessin ou un schéma. Alors dès que j'avais une commande, dès la première conversation, j'ai toujours essayé de faire un croquis d'intention. Très peu de personnes sont capables de comprendre une explication verbale. En revanche, un dessin est parlant pour tout le monde.

TF En parlant de vos moteurs d'influence, on peut dire que vous avez été un précurseur. Quand vous êtes arrivé à Paris, vous avez été directeur de la communication des Galeries Lafayette. Comment en êtes-vous arrivé là? Qu'est-ce qui vous a amené à Paris?

PK Mes professeurs de l'école de Zurich nous conseillaient de finir nos études à l'étranger. J'avais choisi Paris et mon intention était d'aller aux Beaux-Arts. Je m'y suis inscrit. Mes collègues, qui avaient dix ans de plus que moi, finissaient, eux, leur cursus et commençaient à présenter leurs premières expositions; ils me confiaient le design graphique de leurs affiches. J'appliquais ce que la Kunstgewerbeschule de Zurich m'avait enseigné. À partir de là, ils m'ont recommandé et très vite, on m'a confié le logo de NRF (*Nouvelle Revue Française*), des Galeries Lafayette puis de *Elle*.

Les frères Adnet tenaient les écoles d'art de Paris et l'un des deux était directeur artistique des Galeries Lafayette. Il m'a engagé. J'ai tout de suite modifié la typographie. En France, c'était plutôt Didot et Garamond. Venant de Suisse, j'ai introduit les linéaires, comme Futura que j'affectionnais particulièrement. J'ai transformé l'intégralité de ce que l'on appelle le code typographique de ce grand magasin. Aussi, toutes les publicités étaient en dessin noir et blanc dans les quotidiens. J'ai imposé la photographie à la place du dessin. Une véritable révolution pour l'époque!

TF Ce qui est incroyable, c'est qu'on parle des années 1952–1953!

PK Oui, j'avais seulement 24 ans quand ils m'ont nommé directeur artistique.

TF C'est une très grande responsabilité. Vous parlez de typographie: quand vous avez rejoint *Elle* en tant que directeur artistique, dans les années 1950–1959, vous avez aussi cassé ses codes typographiques, faisant preuve d'une liberté extraordinaire. Vous pouvez nous en parler un peu?

PK C'est important de dire que c'est Hélène Lazareff, qui avait travaillé chez Harper's Bazaar à New York avec Alexey Brodovitch, qui m'a confié la direction artistique de *Elle*. Elle attendait de moi que j'opère des modifications importantes. C'est ce que j'ai fait, en commençant par transformer l'équipe et engager des graphistes compétents.

Le Monde ou *Le Figaro* ont un code très précis. Les quotidiens doivent avoir une identité graphique facilement reconnaissable. Contrairement aux journaux, les hebdomadaires ont plus d'intérêt à se renouveler toutes les semaines. Ils sont plus amusants à feuilleter et à découvrir s'ils changent de typo et de styles d'images le plus souvent possible. À contre-courant, j'ai abandonné le gabarit, laissant une liberté totale aux graphistes. Je commençais à prendre plus de photoreporters comme Jeanloup Sieff et Frank Horvat par exemple, à la place des photographes de mode. Dans le *Elle* de l'époque, vous trouvez, dans un même numéro, des photos de Sarah Moon et d'Oliviero Toscani, qui ont des approches complètement opposées.

TF Vous avez aussi introduit la vie, introduit le mouvement dans la photographie de mode pour contrer l'hégémonie de la haute couture. Parlez-nous un peu de cette volonté de casser cet aspect très hiératique.

PK Dans les années 1950, la haute couture française avait une renommée internationale. Beaucoup de couturières copiaient les modèles de Christian Dior ou de Jeanne Lanvin. La bourgeoise argentée allait chez ces couturières et portait du sur-mesure. Quand elle m'a engagé au début des années 1960, la fondatrice du journal *Elle* me disait: «La bourgeoisie et la haute couture, c'est fini. L'avenir, c'est

Q. Peter Knapp (photography and art direction) for *Elle*, August 1961 © Archive Peter Knapp
R. Peter Knapp (photography and art direction) for *Elle*, November 1961 © Archive Peter Knapp

Tatyana Franck in conversation with Peter Knapp
Lausanne, 18 March 2021

Tatyana Franck Peter Knapp, you're a photographer, filmmaker, graphic artist, painter, draughtsman, art director and teacher: you're an image-maker in the truest sense. Today, at the age of 90, you still have extraordinary enthusiasm and a sparkle in your eye. What motivates you? What is the driving force in your life?

Peter Knapp What motivates me is translating ideas into images: trying to transcribe what I think, what I invent, the stories I want to tell through images. I'm an admirer of Charlie Chaplin and Federico Fellini, who produced great visual narratives. I'm a filmmaker and photographer by turns. The concept dictates the tool I use.

When I was still a student, I bought a book about Leonardo da Vinci and the method of painting. It cost a lot of money and turned out to be a disappointment because it mainly dealt with chemistry and how paint is made. Since paint was very expensive at the time, I remember the book recommended using black backgrounds because black was more affordable. But there was one sentence that struck me and is still important to me today: an idea is nothing until it's captured in a design or a pattern. So as soon as I received a commission, right from the first conversation, I've always tried to produce a design sketch. Very few people are capable of understanding a verbal explanation, but a drawing speaks to everyone.

TF   Turning to your influences, it's fair to say you've been a trailblazer. When you arrived in Paris, you were director of communication at Galeries Lafayette. How did you end up there? What brought you to Paris?

PK   My tutors at the school in Zurich advised us to complete our studies abroad. I chose Paris and my plan was to go to the Beaux-Arts. I enrolled there. My colleagues, who were ten years older than me, were already finishing their courses and starting to present their first exhibitions, and they got me to do the graphic design for their posters. I applied what the Kunstgewerbeschule in Zurich had taught me. After that, they soon started recommending me, and I was asked to do the logos for NRF (*Nouvelle Revue Française*), Galeries Lafayette and then *Elle*.

The Adnet brothers ran art schools in Paris and one of them was the art director of Galeries Lafayette. He hired me. I immediately changed the typography. In France, they tended to use Didot and Garamond. Coming from Switzerland, I introduced linears like Futura, which was a particular favourite of mine. I overhauled the entire style guide for that big store. Also, all the advertisements in the daily papers were black-and-white drawings. I insisted on photographs instead of drawings. That was a revolutionary move at the time!

TF   What's unbelievable is that we're talking about 1952–1953!

PK   Yes, I was only 24 when they appointed me art director.

TF   That's a very big responsibility. You mention typography: when you joined *Elle* as art director between 1950 and 1959, you also binned the style guide and demonstrated an extraordinary degree of freedom. Can you tell us a little about that?

PK   It's important to say that it was Hélène Lazareff, who'd worked at Harper's Bazaar in New York with Alexey Brodovitch, who made me art director of *Elle*. She expected me to make big changes. And that's what I did, starting by overhauling the team and hiring some skilled graphic artists.

Le Monde and *Le Figaro* have a very precise style guide. The dailies need a graphic identity that's easily recognisable. Unlike newspapers, weekly magazines have more to gain from changing how they look with each issue. They're more entertaining to browse through and explore if they change their typography and image style as often as possible. I went against the flow by abandoning the template to give the graphic designers complete freedom. I started using more photo reporters such as Jeanloup Sieff and Frank Horvat rather than fashion photographers. In *Elle* at that time you'll find photos by Sarah Moon and Oliviero Toscani, who have completely different approaches, both in the same issue.

TF   You also introduced life and movement into fashion photography to counter the hegemony of *haute couture*. Tell us a little about your desire to get rid of that very hieratic aspect.

PK   In the 1950s, French *haute couture* was internationally renowned. A lot of dressmakers copied the models of Christian Dior and Jeanne Lanvin. Moneyed middle-class women would go to those dressmakers and wear made-to-measure clothing. When she hired me in the early 1960s, the founder of *Elle* told me: "The bourgeoisie and *haute couture* are finished. The future is in ready-to-wear. If I'm involved with a magazine that's selling a million copies I want to be talking to all women, not just one class. I don't want photos that are chic, I want ones that are youthful!" Simple, off-the-peg clothing is inherently less spectacular than what comes from *haute couture*. But when I translate a woman's bearing into movement, I bring her to life. Until then, photos had mostly been taken in the studio and were static. I brought the models out onto the street to emphasise their looks. They'd step off the pavement, walk a few paces up a staircase and then repeat the same movement. Back then, cameras didn't have motor drives, so I used 16 mm movie cameras. If I kept filming for three or four seconds that would give me 84 images! The movements resulted in spontaneous images that didn't look at all posed. At the same time, I aimed to suggest a certain bearing.

TF   You talk about foregrounding vibrancy and youthfulness, and you also broke the mould by using women who were not necessarily models but also "everyday". Tell us about that change and the stir it created.

PK   That wasn't my idea. It came, again, from Hélène Lazareff. "Use your girlfriends!" she told me. I was an admirer of the photographer Irving Penn and his spectacular photographs. It's easy with *haute couture* clothes. In *Elle*, the choices that fashion journalists made led to a new style. The images followed that trend.

TF   Specifically, how did you work on the flatplan for *Elle* magazine?

PK   Every Tuesday morning, at the editorial meeting, all the section editors would be wrangling over who was going to get the most pages. The editor-in-chief would then decide who was to be given what. I had an empty flatplan in front of me. I'd start immediately making watercolour sketches for the subjects that were being suggested. That allowed me to visualise the magazine as a whole and its rhythm. The editor ruled on the choice of clothes depending on whether the pages concerned were going to be in colour or black and white. The art director would then select the photographer on the basis of that, depending on whether the emphasis was on form or chromatic sensibility.

TF   Did you keep the flatplans?

PK   I don't have any of the ones for *Elle*. The Bibliothèque

le prêt-à-porter. Dans mon journal tiré à un million d'exemplaires, je veux m'adresser à toutes les femmes. Et pas seulement à une classe. Je ne veux pas de photos chic mais des photos jeunes!». Le vêtement simple de prêt-à-porter est, en soit, moins spectaculaire que ce qui vient de la haute couture. Mais le comportement de la femme, en le mettant en mouvement, l'anime. Jusque-là, les photos étaient principalement faites en studio, statiques. Moi, je sortais avec les mannequins dans la rue pour souligner leur allure. On descendait du trottoir, on faisait quatre pas sur un escalier, et on répétait le même mouvement. À cette époque, les appareils photographiques n'étaient pas encore équipés de moteur. J'ai donc pris des caméras de cinéma 16 mm. En appuyant trois ou quatre secondes, j'avais déjà 84 images! Ces mouvements donnaient des images spontanées, loin de la pose. J'espérais suggérer en même temps un comportement.

TF   Vous parlez de mettre en avant l'aspect vivant, la jeunesse, vous avez aussi cassé les codes en faisant appel non plus, forcément, à des mannequins, mais à des femmes «de la vie de tous les jours». Parlez-nous aussi de ce changement qui a fait du bruit.

PK   Cette idée ne venait pas de moi mais, encore une fois, d'Hélène Lazareff. «Prends tes copines!» me disait-elle. Moi, j'étais admiratif du photographe Irving Penn et de ses photographies spectaculaires. C'est facile avec un vêtement de haute couture. Dans Elle, les choix qui étaient faits par des journalistes de mode amenaient un nouveau style. Les images suivaient cette tendance.

TF   Concrètement, comment est-ce que vous travailliez à la réalisation du chemin de fer du journal Elle?

PK   Tous les mardis matin, à la conférence de rédaction, tous les chefs de rubrique se bagarraient pour avoir un maximum de pages. Le rédacteur en chef tranchait et faisait la répartition. J'avais un chemin de fer vide devant moi. Immédiatement, je faisais des croquis d'intention à l'aquarelle des sujets proposés. Cela me permettait de visualiser l'ensemble et le rythme du magazine. Le rédacteur déterminait son choix de vêtements selon l'attribution des pages en couleur ou noir et blanc. Le directeur artistique choisissait aussi le photographe en conséquence, selon la mise en valeur de la forme, ou la sensibilité chromatique.

TF   Et vous avez conservé ces chemins de fer?

PK   Du journal Elle, je n'en ai plus. La Bibliothèque nationale de France et le Centre national des arts plastiques (CNAP) à Paris en ont acquis un certain nombre.

TF   La photographie de mode, c'est par essence une photographie appliquée à la commande. Est-ce que vous pouvez nous parler de cette évolution et vous, de votre regard propre?

PK   La photographie de mode est faite pour être imprimée. C'est une commande, c'est donc de l'art appliqué. Une photo de mode pour le journal Vogue a un tout autre esprit que celle réalisée pour le journal Elle. Une photo de mode pour un couturier est très différente d'une publicité. Si le photographe ne comprend pas cette différence, il se trompe. Ici, il ne fait pas de l'art, il travaille pour un client.

La commande que souhaite la majorité des photographes, c'est la photographie de mode. Parce qu'elle laisse une grande liberté dans l'expression visuelle: le magazine de mode ne vend pas directement les vêtements, mais un état d'esprit. Cette photographie est aussi la plus mal payée. Une qualité photographique est attendue. Un catalogue par correspondance, par exemple, attend une photographie informative, où le vêtement est clairement lisible. Nous sommes plus près du document. La photographie de publicité est certainement la plus difficile, car elle réunit toutes les exigences. C'est aussi la mieux rémunérée.

Un journal fait 30 cm de haut. Les photographes ont tendance à présenter des tirages 30 × 40 cm au directeur artistique. Une fois imprimée dans un journal qui est mis en page avec titres et textes, la photographie prend une certaine place. Le choix de la mise en page dépend de la photographie: peut-elle être imprimée en petit parce que son aspect est simple, ou exige-t-elle d'être imprimée en grand parce qu'elle contient beaucoup d'informations qui ne sont pas visibles si la taille de l'image est trop petite?

TF   Par rapport à ces questions d'évolution, à l'époque vous avez pu gagner votre vie grâce aux commandes que vous avez reçues. Aujourd'hui, on sent que les photographes contemporains peinent à avoir des commandes. Une partie de leurs ressources provient des institutions qui les soutiennent et les aident à produire. Comment est-ce que vous voyez cette évolution du métier? Comment l'avez-vous, vous-même, vécue, puisqu'aujourd'hui on peut dire que vous vivez principalement de votre travail créatif, artistique et personnel?

PK   Au départ, nous étions peu de photographes de mode. Tous les jeunes rêvaient de devenir reporter. C'était les débuts de Magnum, leurs modèles, c'étaient Robert Capa, Werner Bischof ou encore Henri Cartier-Bresson. De la photographie humaniste et d'actualité. À l'époque, la photographie de mode ne les attirait pas.

TF   Pour en revenir à cette question, aujourd'hui le métier de photographe de mode a profondément changé et évolué. Vous voyez, je crois intéressant que vous parliez de l'évolution du métier en lui-même.

S.   Peter Knapp, sketch for Elle, no. 921, 1963 © Archive Peter Knapp

T. Peter Knapp (art direction) for *Elle*, no. 944, 1964, Brian Duffy (photography) © Museum für Gestaltung Zürich, Graphics Collection, ZHdK

nationale de France and the Centre national des arts plastiques (CNAP) in Paris acquired some of them.

TF   Fashion photography, by its nature, is applied photography done to order. Can you tell us about that change and your own perspective?

PK   Fashion photography is made to be printed. It's a commission, so it's applied art. A fashion photo for *Vogue* magazine has a completely different flavour from one created for *Elle*. A fashion photo for a dressmaker is very different from an advertisement. Any photographer who doesn't understand that difference is doing it wrong. He isn't making art: he's working for a client.

The kind of commission the majority of photographers want is fashion photography, because it gives you a great deal of freedom in terms of visual expression: a fashion magazine isn't directly selling the clothes, it's selling a state of mind. That kind of photography is also the worst paid. You're expected to deliver photographic quality. A mail-order catalogue, for example, needs an informative photograph that tells you all you need to know about the item of clothing. It's more like a document. Advertising photography is unquestionably the most difficult because it combines all the different requirements. It's also the best paid.

A magazine is 30 cm in height. Photographers tend to approach the art director with 30x40 cm prints. Once it's printed in a magazine where the layout includes titles and texts, the photograph takes up a certain amount of space. The choice of layout takes into account whether a photo can be printed small because it's uncomplicated, or whether it needs to be printed large because it contains a lot of information that can't be seen otherwise.

TF   Coming back to the question of change: in those days you were able to make a living from the commissions you received. Today, you get the impression that photographers are finding it difficult to get orders. Some of their income is from institutions that support them and help them to produce. How do you see that development within the profession? What has been your experience of it, given that today you live mainly from your creative, artistic and personal work?

PK   Initially there weren't many of us fashion photographers. All the youngsters dreamt of becoming reporters. It was the start of Magnum, and their role models were Robert Capa, Werner Bischof and Henri Cartier-Bresson. It was photography about human, topical subjects. Fashion photography didn't appeal to them.

TF   To come back to that question, today the fashion photographer's profession has changed beyond all recognition. I'd like to hear what you have to say about the profession itself evolving.

PK   Nowadays, fashion photography has become a dream for many photographers. Photojournalism has lost its lustre now that news is all over TV and the Internet.

There's too much competition and the newspapers are having a hard time. Fashion designers no longer have the power they used to. The Balenciagas and Courrèges who were imitated the world over have become rare. Fashion journalists have disappeared too. The rules of the game have changed. Photographers don't just want to be witnesses; they want to create for themselves. But that isn't what's expected of them. So they don't get commissions any more. They do creative photography and live in hope that their images will become works of art, sold in galleries and exhibited in museums. You just have to look at it: galleries exhibit sure-fire hits like Avedon and Penn, some of the world's best, and a few others have found a place for themselves, like David LaChapelle and Paolo Roversi. You occasionally see fashion photographs in museums, but they've lost their "fashion" connotation. They've only made it in there because of their photographic and historical value. It's not somewhere a young fashion photographer can hope to end up.

TF   Indeed, what interests us as a museum of photography is to understand the photographer's different crafts. Because for us, there isn't just one photographer: there are many, and understanding their approaches and creative processes is key. When you acquire an image or body of work from a photographer, you're interested in the entirety of their vision. You ask how they view their profession.

PK   Yes, fashion photography has found its way into museums pretty much by accident.

TF   I wouldn't say "by accident", but in any event, as a generalist museum of photography what we're really aiming to do is show the diversity of photography, and fashion photography is part of that.

In the late 1960s, your search for the feminine ideal in fashion photography prompted you to create a body of work that is distinctly personal – I might even say a quest for the infinite – in the form of the sky photographs. Can you tell us about those?

PK   Fashion photography requires us to idealise the world. If you're a creative person, that's not going to satisfy you over the long term. Just for a change, I went up into the sky

PK Aujourd'hui, la photographie de mode est devenue le rêve d'une grande partie des photographes. Le photojournalisme a perdu de sa gloire avec les actualités à la télévision et sur internet.

Il y a trop de candidats et les journaux vont mal. Les créateurs de mode n'ont plus la puissance qu'ils ont eue. Les Balenciaga, Courrèges, imités dans le monde entier, sont devenus rares. La journaliste de mode, elle a disparu aussi. Les règles du jeu ont changé. Les photographes ne veulent plus seulement témoigner, ils veulent créer par eux-mêmes. Mais ce n'est plus ce qu'on attend d'eux. Donc ils n'ont plus de commandes, ils font des photographies créatives et vivent dans l'espoir que leurs images deviennent des œuvres d'art, qu'elles soient vendues dans les galeries et exposées dans les musées. Il faut faire l'analyse: les galeries exposent des valeurs sûres comme Avedon ou Penn, parmi les plus grands du monde, et certains autres ont trouvé une place, comme David LaChapelle ou Paolo Roversi. Dans les musées, nous trouvons exceptionnellement des photographies de mode, mais elles ont perdu leur connotation «mode». Elles y sont entrées uniquement pour leur valeur photographique et historique. Ce n'est pas une place qu'un jeune photographe de mode peut espérer.

TF Effectivement, nous, ce qui nous intéresse en tant que musée, pour la photographie, c'est de comprendre les métiers. Que sont les métiers de photographes? Parce que, pour nous, il n'y a pas un photographe, il y a des photographes, et comprendre leurs démarches et leurs processus créatifs est essentiel. Effectivement, quand on acquiert une image ou un fonds d'un photographe, on s'intéresse à toute sa vision. On se demande comment il pense son métier.

PK Oui, la photo de mode est presque entrée par hasard dans le musée.

TF Je ne dirais pas par hasard, mais en tout cas, notre souhait, en tant que musée généraliste de photographie, c'est vraiment de montrer la diversité de la photographie, et la photographie de mode en fait partie.

Cette recherche, dans la photographie de mode, de l'idéal féminin vous a poussé, à la fin des années 1960, à développer un travail éminemment personnel, une quête, si j'ose dire, de l'infini, que sont ces photographies de ciels. Est-ce que vous pouvez nous en parler?

PK Faire de la photo de mode nous contraint à idéaliser le monde. Ce n'est pas satisfaisant à long terme pour quelqu'un de créatif. Pour créer une rupture, je suis rentré dans le ciel et j'y suis resté vingt ans! En fait, j'ai fait un geste radical en photographiant des ciels bleus par beau temps. Ce travail photographique a abouti à 73 ciels bleus monochromes pris aux quatre coins du monde. Ça a donné une exposition à la Galerie Denise René en 1975, qui s'appelait «Il fait beau». Le résultat était une comparaison de bleus et ma quête de l'infini n'a évidemment pas été satisfaite. Par la suite, j'ai cherché ce qui se passe entre l'infini et moi. Par exemple, le trait d'un avion qui passe. Le vent aussi. En soit, il n'est pas visible. Mais il prend forme quand il déforme un drapeau suisse qui flotte. Je me suis intéressé à saisir en images fixes la déformation de la croix du drapeau dans ce cas-là. Il ne faut pas y voir une déclaration patriotique, mais une recherche formelle. En fait, j'ai fait plusieurs expériences autour du ciel qui m'ont passionné et éloigné de la mode.

TF À propos de vos expériences personnelles, cette réflexion sur les gradations de couleurs Pantone, c'est un travail que vous avez mené au Brésil?

PK On m'a invité à participer à un échange culturel France-Brésil. À Rio, sur la plage, j'ai découvert des jeunes gens se tenant par la main qui entraient ensemble dans la mer. J'ai regardé ce spectacle et j'ai surtout retenu que ces Brésiliens étaient de toutes les couleurs. Cette idée du nuancier est apparue parce que face à cette réalité, le racisme est encore trop présent. Dans une banlieue parisienne, où il y a une belle mixité ethnique, j'ai mis une annonce à la sortie du métro. J'ai ainsi photographié une soixantaine de personnages, aux couleurs de peau très différentes. J'ai mesuré sur chacun cette couleur, d'une façon électrique, toujours au même endroit au milieu du front. Cela m'a donné le code Pantone pour chacun. Le résultat final est une photo qui montre la couleur de la peau accompagné de son code Pantone.

TF Est ce que cette question identitaire est importante pour vous, en tant que Suisse ayant vécu près de 50 ans en France? Comment est-ce que vous percevez cette notion d'identité dans votre travail? Est-ce que cette question a eu une influence dans votre travail?

PK Sûrement. De toute façon, je me suis toujours senti un peu mieux en France qu'en Suisse. Vous voyez, si on est un peu radical, on peut dire qu'en Suisse «ce qui n'est pas interdit est obligatoire.» Ce comportement extrêmement civique est par moment pesant, n'est-ce pas? C'est comme une autoroute qui n'est pas dans un paysage, mais sur un pont et sans barrière. On est dessus ou on est à côté. Et en France, on peut être un peu à côté et ça passe quand même.

TF Vous racontiez à quel point le film a eu très tôt une importance dans votre carrière. Vous nous racontiez cet exemple de la caméra 16 mm utilisée pour vos travaux de mode. Vous avez été très influent dans la réalisation, notamment avec la série *Dim Dam Dom* pour la télévision française. Est-ce que vous pouvez nous en parler?

PK En 1965, la télévision était encore en noir et blanc. Daisy de Galard, rédactrice en chef pour *Elle*, produisait aussi des émissions à la télévision. Elle m'a demandé comment on pouvait amener la mode à la télévision. Je lui ai répondu: ça ne peut pas être la mode! La mode est une information permanente qui se présente en image fixe. La photographie vous laisse le temps de lire l'image à votre rythme. La télévision est une information événementielle, comme le théâtre ou la radio. La durée vous est imposée. Il faut donc amener la mode d'une façon vivante et mouvante, tout en maintenant sa présence à l'écran une vingtaine de secondes au moins, pour que l'information puisse passer. Évidemment, l'image animée m'a toujours intéressé, on peut y exprimer toute sa créativité. J'étais absolument ravi de faire les *Dim Dam Dom,* ça m'amusait beaucoup. Je mettais en scène les mêmes thématiques que dans les magazines féminins. En filmant, on passe facilement d'un plan à un autre, de la silhouette à un gros plan. Il est facile d'agrandir les détails là où à l'inverse, sur l'image fixe, c'est à vous de les trouver.

Daisy de Galard était la première qui permettait l'humour, la dérision et la critique, ce qui était nouveau pour la télévision. J'ai fait ça pendant quatre ou cinq ans, je crois. En tout une quarantaine de films. Puis je suis passé à une autre expérience télévisuelle. J'adore la musique classique et tous les concerts filmés ne montrent que le chef d'orchestre et les musiciens. Ça m'ennuie terriblement... Alors j'ai proposé d'illustrer avec des images les concerts classiques ou de musique contemporaine, dans l'espoir d'augmenter l'audience. On m'a mis en contact avec Pierre Boulez, à qui j'ai raconté mon idée. Il m'a répondu «Mais Peter, si on ne

and ended up staying for twenty years! I made a radical departure by photographing blue skies on fine days. That produced 73 monochrome blue skies taken all over the world, which led to an exhibition at the Galerie Denise René in 1975 called *Il fait beau*. What I ended up with was a comparison of blues, and my quest for the infinite obviously wasn't satisfied. So I set out to find what's going on between the infinite and me. For example, the trail of a passing aeroplane. The wind, too: it's not actually visible itself, but it acquires form when it flutters a Swiss flag. I was interested in capturing a static image of the way it reshapes the cross on the flag. It's not so much a patriotic declaration as a formal experiment. In fact I did a number of experiments with the sky that fascinated me and took me away from fashion.

TF Talking of your personal experiments, that study of the gradations of Pantone shades – was that something you did in Brazil?

PK I was invited to take part in a cultural exchange between France and Brazil. On the beach in Rio I saw young people holding hands and walking into the sea together. I watched them, and what I mainly took away from it is that Brazilians come in all colours. The colour chart idea came about because even in the face of that reality, racism is still all too present. In a suburb of Paris where there's a vibrant ethnic mix I placed an advertisement at the exit from the metro. I photographed about 60 people with very different skin colours. I measured that colour on each of them, electronically, always at the same point in the centre of the forehead, and that gave me the Pantone code for each. The final result is a photo showing each skin colour together with its Pantone code.

TF As a Swiss citizen who's lived in France for almost 50 years, would you say that the question of identity is important to you? How do you see the notion of identity in your work? Has it influenced what you do?

PK Certainly. In any event, I've always felt a bit more at home in France than in Switzerland. You see, if you're a bit radical, in Switzerland it's a case of "what isn't forbidden is compulsory". That attitude of extreme civic responsibility can be a bit burdensome at times, don't you think? It's like a motorway that isn't in the countryside but on a bridge without barriers. You're either on top of it or alongside it. In France you can be a little to one side and it's still OK.

TF You've said how film was important to your career at a very early stage, and you gave us the example of the 16 mm camera you used for your fashion work. You've been very influential in film-making, especially with the *Dim Dam Dom* series for French television. Can you tell us about that?

PK In 1965, television was still in black and white. Daisy de Galard, the editor-in-chief of *Elle*, was also making films for television, and she asked me how we could bring fashion to TV. I told her that it wouldn't be fashion if we did! Fashion is permanent information in the form of a static image. Photography gives you time to read the image at your own speed. Television is event-based information, just like theatre and radio. The duration is imposed on you. So what you need to do is to present fashion in a lively and animated way, while keeping it on screen for at least twenty seconds or so in order to get the information across. Of course, I've always been interested in animated images: they allow you to express your full creativity. I was absolutely delighted to make the *Dim Dam Dom* programmes; it was a lot of fun. I was covering the same topics as in the women's magazines. When you're filming, you can move easily from one plane to another, from silhouette to close-up. It's easy to zoom in on the details whereas, in a static image, you have to pick them out yourself.

Daisy de Galard was the first to allow humour, mockery and criticism, which was new for TV. I did that for four or five years, I think. Around 40 films in all. Then I moved on to another televisual experience. I love classical music, and filmed concerts only ever show the conductor and the musicians. That really annoys me. So I suggested using images to illustrate classical or contemporary music concerts in the hope of increasing the audience. Someone put me in touch with Pierre Boulez and I told him my idea. He said: "But Peter, if people can't see the musicians, we don't get paid! Your idea is a very good one, but it can only ever be a film, it can't be made for television." Two years later, the programme *Musique Graffiti* called me to ask if I wanted to tell the story of the piano from Bach to Béla Bartók. I made 35 films, each just seven minutes long, with the pianist Elizabeth Sombart. In order to film her in an unconventional way, I put her on a rotating platform and positioned six cameramen around her. Each concentrated on one aspect: for one it was her hands, for another it was her face, while others focused on the black lacquer, the instrument, the strings and so on. And then I introduced some other, fairly abstract external views. That was an interesting experiment!

TF You've continued making films all your life. And you're also passionate about art history. Can you tell us about your film on Vincent van Gogh?

PK For me, van Gogh is the most interesting painter of them all. For the film, I wanted to focus on the last two

U. Peter Knapp, Pierre Cardin, 1970 © Archive Peter Knapp

voit pas les musiciens, nous ne sommes pas payés ! Ton idée, c'est très bien, mais ça ne peut être qu'un film, ça ne peut pas être pour la télévision. » Deux ans après, l'émission *Musique Graffiti* m'appelle pour me proposer de raconter l'histoire du piano, de Bach à Béla Bartók. J'ai fait 35 films, dont un de 7 minutes seulement, avec la pianiste Elizabeth Sombart. Pour filmer la pianiste d'une façon inattendue, je l'ai installée sur une plateforme tournante et j'ai placé six cameramen autour d'elle. Chacun d'eux se concentrait sur une partie. Pour l'un, les mains, pour l'autre, le visage, pour les autres les reflets sur la laque noire, l'instrument, les cordes, etc. En plus, j'introduisais d'autres prises de vues extérieures relativement abstraites. Voilà qui était une expérience intéressante !

TF Vous avez, toute votre vie, continué à réaliser des films. Et vous êtes quelqu'un qui est passionné par l'histoire de l'art. Vous pouvez nous parler de votre film sur Vincent Van Gogh ?

PK Van Gogh est pour moi le peintre le plus intéressant qui soit. Pour le film, je voulais me focaliser sur les deux derniers mois de sa vie à Auvers-sur-Oise. Ma motivation principale : je ne supportais plus l'image romanesque du pauvre homme, malade, ivrogne et suicidaire qui n'a jamais vendu une toile. Quelqu'un qui a dormi toute sa vie à l'hôtel et mangé toute sa vie au restaurant n'est pas pauvre ! Son frère, qui appréciait la qualité de sa peinture, l'a soutenu à la fin de sa vie. On peut aussi dire qu'il a acheté toute la production.

À Arles, Vincent van Gogh trouve une méthode de peinture directe en utilisant des tubes de peinture, ce qui lui permet de déposer la matière en touches sur la toile, un peu comme une mosaïque. Il a ainsi peint quatre-vingt tableaux en deux mois à Auvers, dont soixante sont dans les meilleurs musées du monde.

Il était très solitaire. Il faisait des crises de syphilis, qui, à l'époque, était très difficile à diagnostiquer. Il se suicide à 37 ans, mais il n'est pas le seul parmi les artistes. Avec ce film, j'avais envie de rétablir une certaine vérité sur ce personnage fascinant.

TF Vous êtes très attaché à la notion de transmission, de pérennité. Vous avez été enseignant pendant près de quinze ans. Quel impact a eu ce rôle d'enseignant ?

PK Mon collègue Roman Cieślewicz, professeur à l'école Penninghen à Paris, me demande un jour de venir enseigner la conception d'image et la photographie à une classe de terminale. Une grande partie des élèves avait déjà plus de 20 ans. Je n'étais donc plus face à des étudiants, j'étais avec des collègues, voire même avec mes futurs concurrents. On échangeait plutôt qu'autre chose. Surtout, j'invitais les photographes et les cinéastes à la mode à venir intervenir en classe. Les étudiants entendaient des témoignages concrets, de professionnels actuels, avec leurs vécus, leurs soucis, les vraies difficultés du métier. Ces gens communiquaient aussi toute leur passion. Les étudiants étaient vraiment ravis d'être en contact avec la vie réelle. Je me suis découvert enseignant, alors que c'est arrivé au hasard de mes rencontres.

Tout comme mes inspirations pour un nouveau travail. Elles proviennent souvent d'une rencontre fortuite. Un jour, dans un train, j'ai une conversation avec un inconnu qui se trouve être chirurgien d'une clinique spécialisée pour enfants leucémiques. Je lui dis « C'est difficile parce que beaucoup meurent ? ». Il me répond : « Oui, mais la moitié vit ! ». On a finalement collaboré ensemble et réalisé un livre dans lequel j'ai mis en page les lettres et les dessins des enfants malades. L'enseignant de ces élèves hospitalisés les laissait écrire ce qu'ils avaient envie d'exprimer. C'était souvent des critiques sur les docteurs et sur leurs propres parents. Leurs écrits et leurs dessins étaient extrêmement touchants. C'est le projet le plus émouvant que j'ai fait.

TF Justement, l'objet livre, c'est ce qui reste aujourd'hui. Ça a été, pour vous, quelque chose de très important dans votre carrière. Vous avez réalisé plus d'une centaine d'ouvrages. Vous avez été directeur de collection, notamment pour le Centre Pompidou. Vous avez gagné plusieurs prix du meilleur livre suisse. Quels sont pour vous les ouvrages qui ont vraiment eu un rôle particulier dans votre carrière ?

PK A la fin des années 1960, j'ai reçu une formidable demande de l'OMS de Genève pour faire vingt volumes sur la santé. C'était une édition assez populaire et basée sur la prévention. Un peu comme un guide de la bonne santé. Quand j'ai accepté cette commande, j'imaginais que j'allais travailler avec des dessinateurs scientifiques. Mais les délais demandés et le rythme des publications (vingt volumes, dont un sortait toutes les six semaines) rendaient la chose impossible. Les dessinateurs scientifiques mettent un mois pour faire un dessin. Chaque livre devait en contenir une cinquantaine. Alors, j'ai totalement changé d'idée et j'ai confié les croquis d'intention que j'établissais avec les docteurs aux meilleurs illustrateurs du monde. Topor, Folon, en France, Urs Landis, en Suisse, Milton Glaser, aux États-Unis. Ça constitue

V. Peter Knapp (photography and graphic design), *Giacometti. La ressemblance impossible*, Paris: Éditions André Sauret, Paris, 1991 © Museum für Gestaltung Zürich, Graphics Collection, ZHdK

W. Peter Knapp (art direction), Peter Wyss (illustration), "Die Knochen", in: *Das Buch der Gesundheit 5*, Monte Carlo: André Sauret, 1967 © Museum für Gestaltung Zürich, Graphics Collection, ZHdK
X. Peter Knapp (art direction), Hans-Ulrich Osterwalder (illustration), "Zyklus der Verdauung", in: *Das Buch der Gesundheit 6*, Monte Carlo: André Sauret, 1967 © Museum für Gestaltung Zürich, Graphics Collection, ZHdK

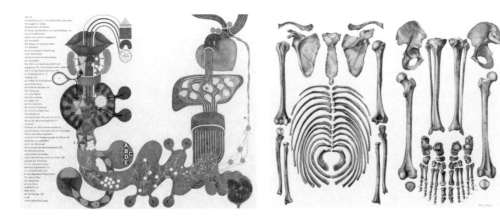

months of his life at Auvers-sur-Oise. My main motivation was that I could no longer accept the romantic image of the poor, sick, drunken and suicidal artist who never sold a canvas. Someone who spent all his life living in hotels and eating in restaurants isn't poor! His brother, who appreciated the quality of his painting, supported him right to the end of his days. You can also say that he bought everything Vincent produced.

In Arles, van Gogh finds a way of painting directly using tubes of paint, which allows him to apply the material onto the canvas in dabs, a bit like a mosaic. So he painted 80 canvases in Auvers over the space of two months, 60 of which are in the world's finest museums.

He was a very solitary person. He contracted syphilis, which was very difficult to diagnose at the time. He committed suicide at the age of 37, but he isn't the only artist to have done that. What I tried to do with that film was restore an element of reality to a fascinating individual.

TF You're very much wedded to the idea of imparting knowledge and ensuring continuity. You were a teacher for nearly 15 years. What impact did that role have?

PK My colleague Roman Cieślewicz, who was a teacher at the Penninghen School in Paris, asked me one day to come and teach image design and photography to a final-year class. Many of the pupils were already more than 20 years old. So I wasn't up against students, I was with colleagues and maybe even my future competitors. More than anything else, we were sharing. In particular, I invited fashionable photographers and filmmakers to come and talk to the class. The students got to hear actual accounts from working professionals, with all their experience and concerns, and about the real difficulties of the profession. So they shared all their passion. The students were absolutely delighted to have contact with real life. I found myself as a teacher during one of my chance meetings.

Inspiration for a new work comes about in the same way – often from a random encounter. One day, in the train, I struck up conversation with a stranger who turned out to be a surgeon at a clinic that specialised in treating children with leukaemia. I asked him: "Is it difficult because many of them die?" He replied: "Yes, but half of them live!" We ended up working together on a book for which I did the layout, containing letters and drawings done by the sick children. Their teacher in the hospital allowed them to write what they wanted. Often, they were critical of the doctors or their own parents. What they wrote and drew was extremely touching. That's the most moving project I've been involved in.

TF The book as object is precisely what we're left with today. It's been very important in your career. You've produced over 100 works. You've been a collection director, notably for the Centre Pompidou. You've won several "Most Beautiful Swiss Books" awards. Which are the works that have played a special role for you in your career?

PK In the late 1960s I received a major commission from the WHO in Geneva to produce 20 volumes on health. It was to be a fairly popular publication based on prevention: a kind of good health guide. When I accepted the commission, I imagined I'd be working with scientific illustrators. But the deadlines and the frequency of publication (20 volumes, one appearing every six weeks) made that impossible. Scientific illustrators take more than a month to produce a drawing. Each book was supposed to include about 50 of them. So I scrapped that idea and I gave the layout sketches I'd put together with the doctors to the world's finest artistic illustrators: Topor and Folon in France, Urs Landis in Switzerland, Milton Glaser in the US. It turned into a remarkable record of illustration at that time. For them, working with doctors was a very unusual experience. That's the publishing project that means most to me.

I'm also very proud of the Collection Art Contemporain, which was created by Alfred Pacquement, who asked me to do the layout for the Centre Pompidou with volumes on Adami, Buraglio, Boltanski and others.

TF You're still very active today. What projects are you working on right now?

PK I've got three projects on the go.

The first is as exhibition curator for the Fondation Maeght in Saint-Paul-de-Vence. In 2017 I produced a book on the five Giacomettis, that amazing family of artists. Isabelle and Adrien Maeght really liked it, and appointed me as curator for the exhibition. It's the first time I've ever done something like that, and I'm really enjoying it.

The second project is a book I'm doing about Slavik, who designed the Drugstores. He fitted out a large number of bistros and restaurants in Paris in the late 1960s. He was THE fashionable interior designer of the day.

un témoignage formidable sur l'illustration de cette époque. Pour eux, c'était tout à fait inhabituel de travailler avec des médecins. C'est le projet éditorial qui me tient le plus à cœur.

Je suis aussi très fier de la Collection Art Contemporain, créée par Alfred Pacquement, qui m'a demandé de la mettre en page pour le Centre Pompidou, avec des volumes sur Adami, Buraglio, Boltanski, etc.

TF Vous êtes toujours très actif, aujourd'hui, sur quels projets travaillez-vous ?

PK J'ai trois projets en cours. Le premier, en tant que commissaire d'exposition pour la Fondation Maeght à Saint-Paul-de-Vence. En 2017, j'ai fait un livre sur les cinq Giacometti, cette incroyable famille d'artistes. L'ouvrage a beaucoup plu à Isabelle et Adrien Maeght, qui m'ont nommé commissaire pour cette exposition. C'est une première expérience dans ma vie, qui me passionne.

Le deuxième projet est un livre que je réalise sur Slavik, qui a conçu les Drugstores. Il a aménagé de nombreux bistrots et restaurants à Paris à la fin des années 1960. C'était le décorateur à la mode.

Enfin, je travaille sur des projets autour de la réunion du Haut-Rhin et du Bas-Rhin. L'attaché culturel du Conseil Régional en Alsace m'a demandé de réfléchir sur des éléments de promotion de ces départements et à des événements pour la fusion. C'est un nouveau projet intéressant.

TF Merci beaucoup Peter Knapp pour ce partage et ce magnifique moment, et surtout, merci d'être une source d'inspiration pour les photographes d'aujourd'hui et les directeurs d'institutions. C'est vraiment un grand bonheur d'échanger avec vous.

PK Ça fait plaisir. Merci !

Tatyana Franck
Directrice, Musée de l'Elysée, Lausanne,
membre de la Commission fédérale du design

Finally, I'm working on some projects related to the merger of the Upper and Lower Rhine *départements*. The cultural attaché at the Regional Council in Alsace asked me to come up with ways of promoting them and some events to bring them together. It's an interesting new project.

TF   Thank you, Peter Knapp, for taking the time to share your thoughts with us, and most of all, thank you for being a source of inspiration for today's photographers and institution directors. It's been a great pleasure to talk to you.

PK   I'm glad to hear it. Thank you!

Tatyana Franck
Director, Musée de l'Elysée, Lausanne,
member of the Swiss Federal Design Commission

Sarah Owens

Dozentin und Forscherin

Professeure et chercheuse   Docente e ricercatrice

Educator and Researcher

Sarah Owens holding *Notebook*, edited by Annamaria Vasvari and herself
photographed by Diana Pfammatter, Zurich, 8 June 2021

Sarah Owens   Design und Vielfalt   von Jonas Berthod

Sarah Owens ist Designdozentin und -forscherin. Ihre Biografie entzieht sich einer gradlinigen Erzählung und lässt sich mit einer Landkarte vergleichen, deren Gebiete durchlässige Grenzen haben. Das zeigt sich auch in den Gründen ihrer Entscheidung, Design zu studieren: Sarah Owens dachte zuerst an eine Karriere als Musikerin, wurde aber Designerin, weil sie so die Begrenzungen der Berufe überschreiten und in vielseitigen Bereichen arbeiten konnte. Ihre Biografie ist eine transdisziplinäre Reise mit Abstechern in Geschichte, Bildung, Film und Literatur.

Nach einem Abschluss in Kommunikationsdesign an der Hochschule Augsburg arbeitete Sarah Owens als Editorial und Corporate Designerin in München und Stuttgart. Die Dotcom-Blase und die Entfremdung zwischen dem Gelernten und der Berufsrealität brachten sie dazu, einen anderen Aspekt ihrer Disziplin zu erforschen. Sie studierte Designgeschichte am Royal College of Art in London, wo sie mit einer Masterarbeit abschloss, in der sie ein Jugendmagazin als textlichen und bildlichen Ausdruck von kulturellen Überzeugungen und gesellschaftlichen Konditionen der 1990er-Jahre analysierte. Aus zunehmendem Interesse für das Fachwissen und die Selbstdefinition von Grafikdesignerinnen und -designern verfasste sie an der University of Reading eine Dissertation zur Beziehung zwischen Alltagsgrafik und professioneller Gestaltungspraxis. Ihre Studien ermöglichten ihr den versierten Umgang mit vielfältigen Diskursen aus der Soziologie, Philosophie und Sozialanthropologie, welche auch für Design relevant sind. Während ihrer Arbeit an der Dissertation erhielt sie ein Stipendium der Akademie Schloss Solitude in Stuttgart, wo sie eine Plattform für Designtheorie entwickelte und eine erweiterte Definition von Design als Zentrum jeder menschlichen Aktivität untersuchte. Die grundlegenden Interessen ihrer Forschung – Fachkenntnis, Wissen, Identität und Othering – kommen in ihrer Karriere immer wieder zum Vorschein.

Sarah Owens dozierte zuerst an Universitäten im Vereinigten Königreich und führte ihre akademische Laufbahn anschliessend während mehr als zehn Jahren an der Zürcher Hochschule der Künste (ZHdK) fort, wo sie zurzeit als Professorin und Leiterin der Fachrichtung Visual Communication arbeitet. Beim Unterrichten, Forschen und Beraten geht sie nach einem untersuchenden Ansatz vor, der aus der Sozialanthropologie stammt: ein Ansatz, der Menschen und Phänomenen in der Begegnung volle Aufmerksamkeit schenkt und zu gemeinsamen Gesprächen anregt. Auch in ihren Vorträgen zu Design und visueller Kultur, in Herausgeberschaften und Beiträgen zur Designtheorie sowie in Forschungsprojekten steht der Dialog im Vordergrund. Dies hat ihre Herangehensweise nachhaltig beeinflusst und sie insbesondere zur Beschäftigung mit dem Einfluss von Mythen und Narrativen des Designs und zur Erforschung von Themen wie Ungleichheit, Normativität und Exklusivität angeregt – Themen, die auch in ihre Lehrtätigkeit einfliessen. In der Ausbildung will sie deshalb die Grenzen des Designs ausweiten und den Studierenden so neue Perspektiven und ein offenes Herangehen an das Designschaffen ermöglichen. Sie setzt sich für eine Bildung ein, die über das Vermitteln von Kompetenzen hinausgeht.

Die Überwindung disziplinärer Grenzen ist Sarah Owens auch bei kulturellen Aktivitäten wie Literatur oder Film wichtig, um ihre Interessen für Bilder, Erinnerung, Geschichte und Marginalisierung zu verknüpfen. Unter anderem ist sie Mitorganisatorin des *Black Film Festival Zurich*. Das jährlich stattfindende Festival setzt den Schwerpunkt auf nichtstereotype Erzählungen über Identität, Geschlecht oder *race*. Sie liest mit Begeisterung alles von Lyrik bis Science-Fiction und nahm auch an einer Serie von Literaturveranstaltungen teil, an denen sie bedeutende zeitgenössische Autorinnen wie Roxane Gay und Taiye Selasi interviewte. Sie brachte in diesen Gesprächen nicht nur ihren akademischen Hintergrund mit, sondern auch ihre eigenen Erfahrungen als Leserin. Ihr Interesse für das ganze Spektrum des Wissens spiegelt sich in ihrem Streben nach Austausch und Kontakt mit einer breiteren Gemeinschaft und dem Verhandeln von Repräsentation und Sichtbarkeit ausserhalb der Universitäten. Diese Aktivitäten sind vielleicht die Essenz von Sarah Owens Laufbahn: die Leidenschaft für ein Wissen, das sich gegen Hierarchien stellt, die Vielfalt feiert und Inklusion anstrebt, aber auch das fortwährende Engagement, um dieses Wissen zu teilen und gemeinsam zu erweitern.

Sarah Owens Le design au pluriel par Jonas Berthod

Sarah Owens est une professeure de design et une chercheuse dont la biographie se refuse à une présentation linéaire : il faut plutôt l'imaginer comme une carte où les régions ont des frontières poreuses. Sa décision d'étudier le design l'illustre bien. Au départ, elle envisageait une carrière de musicienne. Mais elle est devenue designer parce que cela lui permettait de dépasser les frontières professionnelles et d'explorer des domaines variés. Sa biographie peut être caractérisée comme un parcours collaboratif et transdisciplinaire permanent influencé par des incursions dans l'histoire, l'éducation, le cinéma et la littérature.

Après un diplôme en design de communication à l'Université des sciences appliquées d'Augsbourg, Sarah Owens a travaillé comme designer éditoriale et designer d'entreprise à Munich et Stuttgart. L'éclatement de la bulle internet et le décalage entre ce qu'on lui avait enseigné et les réalités de sa profession l'ont ensuite poussée à explorer un autre aspect de sa discipline. Elle a alors étudié l'histoire du design au Royal College of Art de Londres, où elle a consacré son Master à un magazine pour les jeunes en le considérant comme l'expression visuelle et textuelle de croyances culturelles et des conditions sociales des années 1990. Son intérêt croissant pour l'expertise et l'autodéfinition des designers graphiques l'a incitée à étudier dans le doctorat qu'elle a rédigé à l'Université de Reading la relation entre design graphique au quotidien et pratique professionnelle. Ses études supérieures lui ont en outre permis d'approfondir un large éventail de discours qui sont également pertinents pour le design, en particulier la sociologie, la philosophie et l'anthropologie sociale. Alors qu'elle rédigeait son doctorat, elle a obtenu une bourse de l'Académie du château de Solitude à Stuttgart, où elle a développé une plateforme théorique destinée à étudier une définition élargie du design le plaçant au cœur de toute activité humaine. Les éléments fondamentaux qui sous-tendent ses recherches – les notions d'expertise, de connaissance, d'identité et d'altérisation – refont régulièrement surface au fil de sa carrière.

Sarah Owens a donné des cours dans diverses universités du Royaume-Uni avant d'entamer il y a plus d'une dizaine d'années une carrière académique à l'Université des arts de Zurich (ZHdK), où elle est actuellement professeure et responsable du domaine communication visuelle. Dans ses activités d'enseignement, de recherche et de conseil, elle privilégie une démarche d'investigation propre à l'anthropologie sociale : une démarche qui accorde une entière attention aux personnes et aux phénomènes rencontrés et qui nourrit les discussions. Le dialogue occupe également une place essentielle dans ses conférences sur le design et la culture visuelle, dans ses publications et ses articles sur la théorie du design et dans ses travaux de recherche. Cela a durablement déterminé son approche des choses en l'amenant notamment à traiter de l'influence de certains mythes et narratifs du design et à approfondir des thèmes comme l'inégalité, la normativité et l'exclusivité, qui jalonnent aussi son programme d'enseignement. Elle cherche ainsi à élargir les limites du design pour permettre aux étudiantes et étudiants d'être plus ouverts et d'accéder à de nouvelles perspectives. En tant qu'enseignante, elle s'efforce d'établir une voie pédagogique allant au-delà de la transmission de compétence.

Il est également important pour Sarah Owens de dépasser les frontières entre les disciplines dans des activités culturelles telles que la littérature ou le cinéma, ce qui lui permet de conjuguer ses intérêts pour les images, la mémoire, l'histoire et la marginalisation. Elle co-organise en particulier le *Black Film Festival Zurich*, un événement annuel qui accorde la priorité aux narratifs qui traitent sans stéréotypes de l'identité, du genre et de la race. Lectrice avide de tous les genres, de la poésie à la science-fiction, elle a aussi participé à des événements littéraires pour lesquels elle a interviewé des autrices contemporaines reconnues telles que Roxane Gay et Taiye Selasi, apportant dans ces entretiens une perspective nourrie non seulement par les discours académiques mais également, ce qui est tout aussi important, par ses propres expériences de lectrice. Son intérêt pour la connaissance dans toute sa diversité se reflète dans son souci de partager et d'établir des liens dans l'ensemble de la communauté et de traiter des questions de la représentation et de la visibilité hors du cadre de l'université. Ces activités caractérisent sans doute le mieux ce qui constitue le cœur de sa biographie : une passion pour la connaissance sans hiérarchie qui célèbre la pluralité et se concentre sur l'inclusion – et également un engagement tout au long de sa carrière pour le partage et le développement collectif de ce savoir.

Sarah Owens Il design al plurale di Jonas Berthod

Sarah Owens è una docente e ricercatrice di design. La sua biografia sfugge ai consueti profili e può essere paragonata a una mappa le cui regioni hanno confini fluidi. Un aneddoto sulle motivazioni che l'hanno spinta a studiare design ci permette di capire meglio questo paragone: inizialmente, Sarah Owens aspirava a una carriera da musicista, ma la possibilità di spingersi oltre i limiti della professione e di esplorare diversi ambiti l'ha portata a compiere questa scelta. La sua carriera è un percorso interdisciplinare influenzato da storia, istruzione, cinema e letteratura e ricco di continue collaborazioni.

Dopo la laurea in design della comunicazione all'Università di Scienze Applicate di Augusta, Sarah Owens ha lavorato come designer editoriale e aziendale a Monaco e a Stoccarda. Avendo assistito alla Bolla delle Dot-com e percepito il divario tra la formazione e la realtà lavorativa, ha deciso di esplorare un altro aspetto della disciplina, la storia del design, iscrivendosi al Royal College of Art di Londra. L'oggetto della sua tesi di laurea magistrale è una rivista per giovani, analizzata come manifestazione testuale e visiva della cultura e delle condizioni sociali degli anni Novanta. L'interesse crescente verso le competenze dei designer grafici e il loro processo di autodefinizione l'ha spinta a scrivere una tesi di dottorato all'Università di Reading incentrata sulla relazione tra la grafica comune e il design professionale. Grazie agli studi universitari ha acquisito dimestichezza con molte materie attinenti al design, quali ad esempio la sociologia, la filosofia e l'antropologia sociale. Durante il dottorato è divenuta inoltre membro dell'Akademie Schloss Solitude di Stoccarda, dove ha sviluppato una piattaforma per la teoria del design che analizza globalmente questa disciplina, intesa come il fulcro di ogni attività umana. Gli interessi alla base della sua ricerca, tra cui i concetti di competenza, conoscenza, identità e Altro, riemergono continuamente nel corso della sua carriera.

Sarah Owens ha insegnato in diverse università del Regno Unito prima di intraprendere la carriera accademica alla Zürcher Hochschule der Künste (ZHdK), dove lavora da oltre un decennio ed è attualmente responsabile del ciclo di studi in visual communication. Negli ambiti dell'insegnamento, della ricerca e della consulenza si serve di un approccio esplorativo che è tipico dell'antropologia sociale e dedica piena attenzione alle persone e ai fenomeni incontrati, stimolando un discorso comune. Il dialogo è l'elemento centrale anche nelle sue lezioni sul design e la cultura visiva, nei progetti editoriali, negli scritti sulla teoria del design e nei progetti di ricerca. Molti di questi progetti hanno influenzato indelebilmente il suo metodo di insegnamento, portandola soprattutto a mettere in discussione l'influenza esercitata dai miti e dalla narrativa sul design e ad approfondire altri concetti quali la disuguaglianza, la normatività e l'esclusività. Il suo obiettivo nell'insegnamento è ampliare gli orizzonti del design, così da offrire agli studenti e alle studentesse nuove prospettive e un approccio libero alla materia. Come docente si impegna a favore di un percorso formativo che vada oltre l'insegnamento di competenze.

Sarah Owens traspone la stessa filosofia basata sull'assenza di confini fra le discipline anche nelle diverse attività culturali, letterarie e cinematografiche, coniugando così tra loro temi di suo interesse quali la memoria, la storia e l'emarginazione. È inoltre co-organizzatrice del *Black Film Festival Zurich*, un evento annuale che mette in risalto rappresentazioni non stereotipate dell'identità, del genere e della razza. Avida lettrice di qualsiasi genere, dalla poesia alla fantascienza, Sarah Owens ha partecipato a una serie di eventi letterari in cui ha intervistato scrittrici contemporanee come Roxane Gay e Talye Selasi, servendosi della sua esperienza accademica e dell'altrettanto importante esperienza di lettrice per offrire una prospettiva informata sull'argomento. Il suo approccio pluridisciplinare riflette il suo desiderio di condividere ed entrare in contatto con il resto della comunità affrontando questioni di rappresentanza e visibilità al di là dell'ambito accademico. Forse sono proprio questi elementi a definire l'essenza della biografia di Sarah Owens: la passione per un sapere inclusivo, diversificato e libero da ogni gerarchia, ma anche l'impegno totale della sua carriera nel voler condividere e sviluppare insieme questo sapere.

Sarah Owens   Design in the Plural   by Jonas Berthod

Sarah Owens is a design educator and researcher whose biography resists neat narratives: it is best imagined as a map whose regions have porous borders. An anecdote on her decision to study design illustrates this well. Initially, she thought of a career as a musician. However, she became a designer instead, because it allowed her to cross professional boundaries and investigate a diversity of fields. Her biography is characterised by an ongoing collaborative and transdisciplinary journey influenced by incursions into history, education, film and literature.

After graduating from the University of Applied Sciences Augsburg with a degree in communication design, Sarah Owens worked as an editorial and corporate designer in Munich and Stuttgart. The dotcom crash and a disconnect between what she had been taught and the realities of the profession encouraged her to explore another aspect of the discipline. She studied History of Design at the Royal College of Art in London, where her MA dissertation considered a youth magazine as a textual and visual manifestation of cultural beliefs and social conditions during the 1990s. A growing interest in graphic designers' expertise and self-definition motivated her to pursue a PhD at the University of Reading which examined the relationship between everyday graphic design and professional practice. Her graduate studies enabled her to become well-versed in a wide range of discourses relevant to design, including sociology, philosophy and anthropology. While completing her PhD, she also became a Fellow of the Akademie Schloss Solitude in Stuttgart, where she developed a platform for design theory investigating an extended definition of design as the heart of every human activity. The underlying interests in her research – notions of expertise, knowledge, identity and othering – would constantly resurface throughout her career.

Sarah Owens lectured at universities in the UK before developing an academic career over more than a decade at Zurich University of the Arts (ZHdK), where she is currently Professor and Chair of Visual Communication. In teaching, research and consulting, she adopts an inquiry-based approach that borrows from anthropology: one that attends closely and commits fully to the people and phenomena she encounters, thus allowing for joint conversations to unfold. She has edited and contributed to several volumes on design research and theory and has spoken widely on design and visual culture. She has also participated in or led more than a dozen research projects. Many of these had lasting influences on her approach to education, notably leading her to question the influence of myths and narratives within design and to consider notions of inequality, normativity and exclusivity, topics she included in her curricula. Her aim within design education is therefore to expand the boundaries of design so that students gain new perspectives and an openness to the field. As an educator, she strives to create an educational path that goes beyond teaching skills.

Sarah Owens brings the same boundaryless ethos to cultural activities including literature and film, which allow her to connect more of her interests in images, memory, history and marginalisation. Amongst others, she co-organises the *Black Film Festival Zurich*, an annual event prioritising non-stereotypical narratives around identity, gender and race. An avid reader of everything from poetry to science fiction, she also took part in a series of literary events in which she interviewed acclaimed contemporary authors such as Roxane Gay and Taiye Selasi, conversations to which she brought a perspective informed not only by academic discourses but, just as importantly, by her own experiences as a reader. Her consideration for the full spectrum of knowledge reflects her desire to share and connect with the wider community, addressing issues of representation and visibility outside the university. These activities perhaps define the core of Sarah Owens's biography: a passion for knowledge that is anti-hierarchical, celebrates plurality and focuses on inclusion, but also a career-long engagement to sharing and collectively building that knowledge.

Jonas Berthod
Grafiker, Forscher und Dozent, London (UK)
Designer graphique, chercheur et enseignant, Londre (UK)
Designer grafico, ricercatore e insegnante, Londra (UK)
Graphic designer, researcher and lecturer, London (UK)

Sarah Owens

Education

- 2012 University of Reading (UK), PhD in Typography and Graphic Communication
- 2006 Royal College of Art / Victoria & Albert Museum, London (UK), MA (RCA) in History of Design
- 2001 University of Applied Sciences Augsburg (DE), graduate diploma in Communication Design

Selected positions

- 2020– President, Swiss Design Network (SDN); board member since 2016
- 2014– Professor of Visual Communication and Visual Cultures; chair of subject area, head of MA programme and research unit in Visual Communication at Zurich University of the Arts (ZHdK)
- 2009–16 Co-head of BA in Visual Communication; lecturer for design theory at ZHdK
- 2009 Fellowship / artist residency at Akademie Schloss Solitude, Stuttgart (DE)
- 2006–07 Lecturer at London Metropolitan University and University College for the Creative Arts Rochester (UK)
- 2005 Curatorial assistant at Victoria & Albert Museum, London (UK)
- 2004 Designer at Burda Yukom, Munich (DE)
- 2002–03 Freelance editorial designer
- 2002 Designer at Süddeutsche Zeitung Magazin, Munich (DE)
- 2001–02 Designer at Strichpunkt Design, Stuttgart and Munich (DE)
- 2000 Assistant at Surface Gesellschaft für Gestaltung, Frankfurt (DE)

Selected research projects

- 2017–20 "Cache" and "Aether", co-project lead, consultant and project partner, in cooperation with ETH Zurich
- 2016–18 "Dynamic branding for cultural institutions", project lead and consultant, in cooperation with Museum Rietberg Zurich
- 2016–20 "Swiss graphic design and typography revisited", co-applicant and subproject lead, in cooperation with six Swiss universities
- 2014–15 "Art.School.Differences", co-researcher, in cooperation with two Swiss universities
- 2012–14 "Wolfgang Weingart: Typography in context", research associate, in cooperation with the Design Museum Zurich
- 2005–08 "Designing Modern Germany", research associate at the Royal College of Art, London (UK)

Selected conferences and symposia

- 2021 "Design as Common Good", conference co-chair, held at SUPSI and HSLU
- 2018 "Beyond Change", conference co-chair, held at Academy of Art and Design Basel
- 2013 "Design Unfolds: Contemporary Creative Strategies from Appropriation to Collaboration", symposium organisers, held at ZHdK
- 2011 "Making / Crafting / Designing", organised with Björn Franke, held at Akademie Schloss Solitude, Stuttgart (DE)

Selected cultural events

- 2016– *Black Film Festival Zurich*, co-founded with Rispa Stephen and Ania Mathis
- 2019 "Gathering Blossoms under Fire", LUMA Westbau Zurich, organised with Brandy Butler and Tina Reden
- 2018 "Black Madonna: a Black Feminist She perspective", Kunstmuseum Basel, organised with Brandy Butler and Tina Reden
- 2017–19 Conversations with Roxane Gay, Reni Eddo-Lodge and Taiye Selasi at Literaturhaus Zurich and Openair Literatur Festival Zurich
- 2017 "Schwarz und Frau: Unbeachtete Geschichte(n)", Filmpodium Zurich, organised with Rispa Stephen
- 2010 "Copy this magazine", Kunstraum Lothringer 13, Munich (DE), organised with Birgit Merk
- 2006 Workshop for the exhibition "Undercover Surrealism", Hayward Gallery, London (UK)

Selected publications

2021 *Swiss Graphic Design Histories*, eds. D. Fornari, R. Lzicar, S. Owens, M. Renner, A. Scheuermann and P.J. Schneemann, Scheidegger & Spiess

2021 "New perspectives on Swiss graphic design", *Design Issues* 37/1, eds. D. Fornari, R. Lzicar, S. Owens, M. Renner, A. Scheuermann and P.J. Schneemann

2020 "Keep feeling fascination: design and open enquiry", in: *Not at Your Service*, eds. B. Franke and H. Matter, Birkhäuser

2019 "Undoing design. Odprojektować projectowanie", *Formy Journal of Design* 1

2019 "Foreword", in: *notamuse: A New Perspective on Women Graphic Designers in Europe*, eds. S. Baum, C. Scheer and L. Sievertsen, Niggli

2019 "On the professional and everyday design of graphic artifacts", in: *Design Culture*, eds. G. Julier et al., Bloomsbury

2018 *94 Strange Sensations: A Dictionary of the Unseen*, eds. S. Owens and B. Franke, Zurich University of the Arts

2013 *Design exhibited*, OnCurating.org 17, eds. B. Meltzer, T. von Oppeln and S. Owens

2012 *Design is Ordinary: Lay Graphic Communication and its Relation to Professional Graphic Design Practice.* University of Reading

2009 "Visual continuity and innovation in editorial design practice", in: *Design and Creativity*, eds. G. Julier and L. Moor, Berg

2008 *Yes Logo: 40 Years of Michael Peters Branding, Design and Communication*, Black Dog Publishing

2006 "Electrifying the alphabet", *Eye Magazine* 62

Selected talks and panels

2020 "Making and unmaking expert knowledge in design", speaker, European Association for STS, Prague (CZ)

2020 "The in/visible woman: thoughts on representation, presence and the gaze", speaker, ETH Zurich

2019 "Typografie meets Kunst", panellist, Staatsgalerie Stuttgart (DE)

2019 "The dynamics of graphic design practice", speaker, University of Illinois at Chicago (USA)

2019 "A woman's work", panellist, Kunstgewerbemuseum Dresden (DE)

2018 "Explorative design", speaker, Kraków Academy of Fine Arts (PL)

2018 "Madonna – transversal figure, image and icon", panellist, Kunstmuseum Basel

2018 "Whose gaze? Questioning the representation and visibility of blackness", speaker, Academy of Fine Arts Vienna (AT)

2017 "Software as co-designer", speaker, DHBW Ravensburg (DE)

2016 "The world in signs and images", panellist, Museum Rietberg Zurich

2015 "The graphic design canon: when history gets too neat", speaker, AGI Open Conference Biel

2015 "Click to add title: The politics of DIY graphics", speaker, University of Applied Arts Vienna (AT)

2014 "On professional and everyday design practices", speaker, Design School Kolding (DK)

2011 "12 pt. Times New Roman", speaker, ATypI Conference, Reykjavík (IS)

2010 "But, is it design?", speaker, University of Nicosia (CY)

2009 "A study of lay graphic communication", speaker, University of California at Berkeley and Stanford University (USA)

2007 "Locating culture: a reassessment of CCCS models", speaker, University of East London (UK)

2007 "In a league of its own? The jetzt magazine", speaker, University of Macedonia (GR)

2007 "Identity amongst contemporary German youth", speaker, University of Exeter (UK)

2006 "The evolution of type: mutant typography", speaker, Delft University of Technology (NL)

2006 "Electronic typography", speaker, Parsons The New School of Design / Cooper Hewitt National Museum of Design, New York (USA)

CHAPTER TEN

On the professional and everyday design of graphic artefacts

Sarah Owens

Introduction

Graphic design is – in contrast to more rigidly controlled occupations in fields such as medicine or law – a highly permeable profession. It allows flexible career paths, and is more often than not open to outsiders or self-taught designers. Although there exist numerous professional organizations in design, the field lacks strict licensing procedures or those of penalizing misconduct that may end careers (Julier 2008: 44). In graphic design, this circumstance grants employers and clients a relatively high level of freedom when hiring or commissioning. Thus, even the non-formally trained designer, if applying with an interesting portfolio, has a real chance of entering the professional sphere.

An increased access to professional tools, such as desktop publishing software, has also made it easier for non-formally trained designers to enter the profession. At the same time, it has allowed everyday (i.e. non-professional and non-expert) designers to produce graphic artefacts on their own and for their own use. These technological changes are accompanied by a more general opening up of design towards other disciplines and the public, as evident in the participatory design movement since the 1970s, or more recently through design thinking and design for social innovation. Our visual world thus always contains both professional and everyday design, and the forms in which everyday design has become visible are multiplying

auch in der frühen Menschheitsgeschichte. In seinen Büchern „Why We Cooperate" und „Origins of Human Communication" erklärt Michael Tomasello, dass der Wunsch zur Zusammenarbeit und der evolutionäre Vorteil, den sie bietet, unsere heutigen, komplexen Kommunikationsformen hervorgebracht haben. Sie werden durch drei Bedingungen unterstützt: erstens durch eine Theory of Mind; zweitens durch eine beiderseitige Aufmerksamkeit und gemeinsame Ziele, die es uns erlauben, koordiniert und mit klaren Rollen und Regeln zu arbeiten; und drittens durch einen gemeinsamen konzeptuellen Hintergrund, der die Grundlage für Interpretation bietet. All dies ermöglicht es uns, kommunikative Inhalte wie Gesten, Worte oder Bilder zu interpretieren und die Reaktionen anderer auf das, was wir sagen oder tun, vorherzusagen.

  Tomasello gründet sein Argument auf der Annahme, dass Menschen grundsätzlich prosozial und altruistisch sind. Da Altruismus – die Bereitschaft zu Kooperation und Hilfe – angeboren ist, zeigt er sich bereits bei kleinen Kindern. Aus evolutionärer Sicht sind wir auf prosoziales Verhalten angewiesen, da es unser Überleben sichert: In der frühen Menschheitsgeschichte brauchten wir andere, die uns bei der Jagd oder der Nahrungsbeschaffung unterstützten, und wir brauchten andere, die bereit waren, mit uns notwendige Ressourcen wie Unterkunft, Werkzeuge und Informationen zu teilen.

  Im Alter von etwa zwölf Monaten beginnen Kinder, symbolische Gesten zu verwenden, und treten damit in eine kollektive symbolische Realität ein. Sie beginnen, absichtlich auf Dinge zu zeigen, was darauf hinweist, dass sie das Zeigen als altruistische, kommunikative Geste verstehen, die darauf abzielt, Informationen zu teilen. In diesem Alter lernen Kinder auch, auf Dinge zu zeigen, die nicht unmittelbar wahrnehmbar sind. Dadurch löst sich der Gegenstand, auf welchen das Kind hinweisen will, aus der physischen Umgebung und verlagert sich auf eine mentale Ebene. Mit zunehmendem Alter ist das Kind in der Lage, seinen Bezugsrahmen immer mehr zu erweitern und sich damit vom Unmittelbaren zu entfernen, bis es in der Lage ist, über das Immaterielle,

58 **Movement**
59 **Mystery**

60 **Obscure**
61 **Open**
62 **Operate**
63 **Opinion**
64 **Opposite**

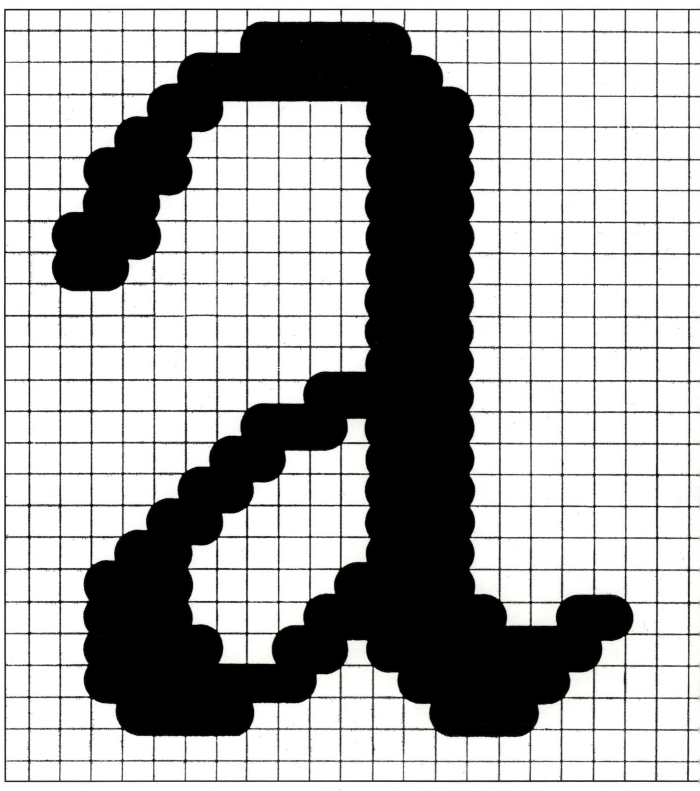

ESSAY / ELECTRONIC TYPE
BY SARAH OWENS

ELECTRIFYING THE ALPHABET

It is customary to start working on images by beginning with an image (or several). You look at the image, question it, wrestle with it, surrender to it, get fed up with it and then begin anew, hopefully with a new perspective. Slowly, the image reveals its layers. And you, you hope that all of its layers will be revealed so that you can claim that you have understood the image in all its facets.

But what do you do with the unseen image? This image hides all of its layers. Its purpose is to not reveal itself to you. It appears (maybe in your mind, maybe on a screen, maybe in conversation), but then vanishes immediately, avoiding your desperate grasp. And you, you feel that you have somehow been cheated.

We started our conversation about unseen images by discussing a desire – the recurrent desire of humankind to connect via images with something that is unknown or imperceptible. The large geoglyphs created by the ancient Nazca culture in Peru have religious significance, they mark altar sites and processions, and can only be seen from

PART I   EDUCATION

All too often, we say what we hear others say. We think what we're told that we think. We see what we're permitted to see. Worse! We see what we're told that we see.—Octavia Butler [i]

We live in times when we are reminded daily of the possible collapse of environmental, social, political and economic systems. At the same time, there is a feeling that the world has become exceedingly complex: although we are able to access vast quantities of information, it seems increasingly difficult to comprehend the interconnectedness of our lives. This feeling of a growing complexity has, however, accompanied humankind throughout history. With our ongoing externalisation of human capacities, we have been trying to keep up with the technologies that were originally meant to unburden us. And although our desire for wealth and comfort exceeds the availability of natural resources, we have been striving to multiply our systems of production, creating precarious networks of labour. We seek knowledge, but become overwhelmed by the amassment of data and its infinite linkages. The current remedy for perceived complexity is to have computing technologies quantify every aspect of our lives. Quantification promises control—but also impacts our view of the world:

> "The issue may not be so much the extent to which the world is unpredictable as the extent to which we are disturbed by its unpredictability. [...] the use of technology has not, in fact, made the

---

[i] Octavia Butler, *Parable of the Talents* (New York: Seven Stories Press, 1998), 277.

[ii] Stephen Rowland, *The Enquiring University: Compliance and Contestation in Higher Education* (Maidenhead: Open University Press, 2006), 6.

world a more predictable or safe place. But perhaps a more technologically oriented way of thinking has made us more averse to unpredictability and its consequent risk."

In the field of design, the aforementioned aversion to risk finds expression in the idea that design is a process of problem-solving. This idea suggests that complex issues can be reduced to distinct, neatly compartmentalised problems for which an appropriate method must be found, and whose application will result in a fitting solution. Put more provocatively, this means that designers frame problems as design problems that necessitate design methods and produce design solutions. And even though many parts of the design process escape quantification, the narrative of problem-solving suggests control, with volatile aspects of the process ideally receding into the background. By solving the problem, the problem disappears … because it has been replaced by the solution. This latter notion, however, brings with it conceptual dilemmas, especially when tackling complex issues. For instance: when exactly has awareness for an issue been achieved? When exactly has society been changed?

The unknown, [...] the unforetold, the unproven, that is what life is based on. Ignorance is the ground of thought. Unproof is the ground of action. [...] The only thing that makes life possible is permanent, intolerable uncertainty; not knowing what comes next. —Ursula K. LeGuin

Ursula K. LeGuin, *The Left Hand of Darkness* (New York: Ace Books, 1969), 75.

№ ✼ 00093

«We are gorgeously contradictory in our epistemologies.»
Elizabeth Alexander

«The resources available to us for benign access to each other, for vaulting the mere blue air that separates us, are few but powerful: language, image, and experience, which may involve both, one, or neither of the first two. Language (saying, listening, reading) can encourage, even mandate, surrender, the breach of distances among us, whether they are continental or on the same pillow, whether they are distances of culture or the distinctions and indistinctions of age or gender, whether they are the consequences of social invention or biology. Image increasingly rules the realm of shaping, sometimes becoming, often contaminating, knowledge. Provoking language or eclipsing it, an image can determine not only what we know and feel but also what we believe is worth knowing about what we feel.»
Toni Morrison

«The unknown, [...] the unforetold, the unproven, that is what life is based on. Ignorance is the ground of thought. Unproof is the ground of action. ...The only thing that makes life possible is permanent, intolerable uncertainty; not knowing what comes next.»
Ursula K. LeGuin

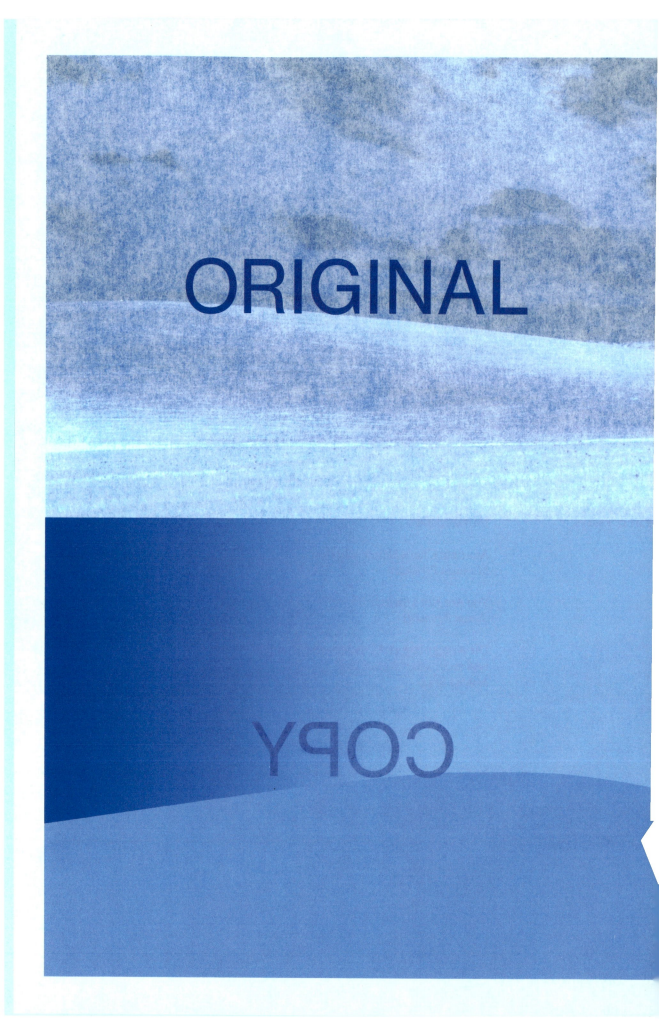

Despite the fact that designers seldom work alone and never create without external influences, the myth of the individual creative genius still looms large in many design disciplines. At the end of the 20th century in particular, certain designers were granted celebrity status—their works were praised in monographs, films and exhibitions based on the idea of extraordinary individual achievement.

During the past few years the notion of the creative genius has, however, been increasingly called into question, not least due to the realization that designers always also profit from the creative work of others. Digital technology has facilitated access to artistic ideas and concepts, as well as to visual and audio content that can be effortlessly copied, modified and combined. Moreover, the idea that only collaborative efforts are able to address the increasingly complex problems resulting from social, ecological and economic change has found a growing number of supporters. As a

Foreword
Sarah Owens

Narratives are powerful, they shape how we make sense of the world. But as the novelist Chimamanda Ngozi Adichie has reminded us, there lies a danger in depending on narratives and stories that present a view that is too narrow. This is because a limited, one-dimensional story brings forth and supports problematic stereotypes, thus claiming priority over more nuanced accounts. "One story become[s] the only story."[1] As graphic designers, we pride ourselves in our storytelling abilities, but often do not pay enough attention to the stories we propagate about ourselves. These are stories about who is recognized as a graphic designer and who is not, who is seen as deserving of accolades and who is not, who is said to have produced noteworthy work and whose work is seen as insignificant, or who is seen as belonging into the graphic design canon, our list of great achievements and role models.

A limited, though still highly popular, story is the following: A great graphic designer is a young man, dynamic, charismatic, white, able-bodied, middle- or upper-class, with no financial worries; who devotes his life to graphic design, defines his own way of working, creates masterpieces and develops a signature style; gets discovered, supported, invited; establishes his own studio and/or teaches, thus influencing subsequent generations; publishes monographs and is interviewed in design magazines; becomes a member of one or several professional organizations; is invited to exhibit work in galleries or museums or at biennials; speaks regularly at conferences; stars in documentaries; and as a consequence, starts being part of graphic design history by being included in the disciplinary canon.

This is a story of success, and in order to make the story more interesting, obstacles are mentioned that need to be overcome in order to heighten this achievement. They include difficult clients, technological breakdowns, maybe even admitting to phases of failing or not being inspired. Obstacles not likely to be included in this story, because they are not likely to be encountered by the designer described above, are: having work disregarded by others since they assume your career will never advance because you will be "distracted" by having a family; being attributed and assigned only certain tasks or topics because other people assume this is what you are "naturally" interested in; being told that your behavior is irritating because it does not conform with the role society has assigned you; having your work considered "good for someone like you", but not "universal" enough to be truly excellent and timeless; or the feeling of resignation following yet another unsuccessful attempt at a place within a professional world that historically did not intend on including you.

This simple story is, however, one that continues to fascinate and exert influence. It implicitly guides those who hire designers when they sort their "to invite" and "to reject" piles of applications. It influences students in their opinion of which lecturers or professors they more readily regard as competent. In turn, it guides those who teach in what they

---

1 Chimamanda Ngozi Adichie, "The Danger of a Single Story", TED Global, July 2009.

A. "On the professional and everyday design of graphic artefacts", in: *Design Culture. Objects and Approaches*, edited by Guy Julier, Mads Nygaard Folkmann, Niels Peter Skou, Hans-Christian Jensen and Anders V. Munch (2019)
B. "Altruismus. Zusammenarbeit. Kommunikation", in: *BA MA Visual Communication* (2020)
C. *94 Strange Sensations. A Dictionary of the Unseen*, edited by Björn Franke and Sarah Owens, designed by Ronny Hunger (2018)
D. "Electrifying the alphabet", in: *Eye, the International Review of Graphic Design*, No. 62 (2006)
E. "The Unseen Image", in: *94 Strange Sensations. A Dictionary of the Unseen* (2018)
F. "Keep feeling fascination: design and open enquiry", in: *Not at Your Service. Manifestos for Design*, edited by Björn Franke and Hansuli Matter (2020)
G. *Design Unfolds. Contemporary Creative Strategies from Appropriation to Collaboration*, symposium, announcement designed by Christian Lange and Johannes Bissinger (2013)
H. *Notebook*, edited by Annamaria Vasvari and Sarah Owens (2020)
I. *Copy Hommage Parody Détournement Sampling Readymade Original*, edited by Sarah Owens, designed by Romy Strasser (2017)
J. "Foreword", in: *notamuse. A New Perspective on Women Graphic Designers in Europe*, edited by Silva Baum, Claudia Scheer, and Lea Sievertsen (2019)

Vera Sacchetti in conversation with Sarah Owens
Basel / Zurich, 10 March 2021

Vera Sacchetti   Sarah, I wanted to start the conversation by introducing you a little bit. You are a design educator with a very international background and outlook. Could you tell us about how you got to where you are now, based in Zurich and teaching for the last decade at the Zurich University of the Arts (ZHdK), where you head the Visual Communication department?

Sarah Owens   I studied communication design in Germany and worked as an editorial and corporate designer for a while. Going into design education was not on my horizon at that moment. At one point, there was a financial crisis that resulted from the "dotcom bubble" bursting – people had invested too much into Internet companies. So I was hopping from one publishing house to the next, and from one studio to the next. Then I thought that since I had always wanted to do graduate studies, this would be the right time. I applied to the Royal College of Art and V&A (Victoria & Albert Museum) in London to study History of Design. There I heard about how design can be viewed, and how design has been viewed in history. It was really about coming to see design as a cultural expression. I also started to read into sociology and cultural theory, and this expanded my idea of what design is. My aim was to figure out why designers do the things that they do, and why they are educated in the way that they are. The next step was doctoral studies, which was self-evident because at the time I did not want to return to practising design. Also, I thought doctoral studies would be the best way to go forward in learning more about the design profession. After studying for the PhD for several years, I decided that academia was the right way to go and applied for jobs. Design education was perfect as it allowed me to bridge theory, practice and history. It enabled me to connect design to other disciplines, to talk with young designers about the role of design and what they want to change. It was an environment to which I could contribute all the interests that I had accumulated over the years. This path sounds very straightforward, but design education was not a career goal for me from the start. It was more that one thing led to another, and that I was always just very interested in and curious about certain things.

vs   Your work in Zurich has certainly been visionary and in part, that is also what this award celebrates. I'm sure you'll agree that what you've been doing at the ZHdK is fundamentally breaking down barriers between design academia as an ivory tower, and trying to reach out and mentor students to understand design as a discipline that can be fundamentally more powerful than what the canon defined for it in the 20th century. You've been there now for a decade. You've had different roles in the department and you head the MA in Visual Communication as well as the Visual Research Unit, which speaks to your interest in design research. I'd like to go back briefly to your trajectory, which hasn't been linear but rather punctuated with very interesting turning points. First of all, your fellowship at the Akademie Schloss Solitude in Stuttgart in 2009, which for you was also a way to make space for a variety of ideas that you were already thinking about. Could you tell us a little about that?

so   In 2009, I had just finished writing a book, I was two years into my PhD and busy with a lot of things. The fellowship at Akademie Schloss Solitude was therefore a very welcome disruption. There was no necessity to produce anything, so I had time to read into philosophy and anthropology, and talk with people from the fine arts, architecture, music, dance, etc. It provided a space to breathe and depart from a cycle where I had been going from one deadline to the next, trying to find my way as an academic. Suddenly I had the freedom to just let ideas emerge. I also realised that I had a very disciplinary perspective, so I was looking at design as a designer. That's how I was trained: I had studied design history, so of course I stayed within the design discourse. But I had the feeling that a lot of disciplines or fields talk about design, and don't necessarily frame it in this way. As a result, and together with Björn Franke who was also a fellow, I organised a symposium at Schloss Solitude two years later. We wanted to look at design as a fundamental human activity and take a very interdisciplinary approach, for instance to see how we as humans design ourselves. We invited speakers from different fields to talk about design. Our aim was to make connections between these various fields, to open up the discussion and take a broader perspective.

vs   I find that very interesting: this idea of lack of outcomes and not being burdened by the constant pressure of academia and design itself to constantly produce; that you had an open space where new ideas could emerge in an interdisciplinary context. Could you tell us about how that understanding, and the understanding you previously mentioned that connects to the social sciences, all came together in your PhD research?

so   Sure. I did my PhD at the University of Reading and explored a topic that came out of my MA thesis. I was very interested in what professional designers would call

K.   "Design is Ordinary", doctoral research at the University of Reading, 2012

Vera Sacchetti im Gespräch mit Sarah Owens
Basel / Zürich, 10. März 2021

Vera Sacchetti Sarah, ich möchte dich zuerst kurz vorstellen. Du bist Designdozentin und hast einen sehr internationalen Hintergrund und Ansatz. Du lebst in Zürich und unterrichtest seit zehn Jahren an der Zürcher Hochschule der Künste (ZHdK), wo du die Fachrichtung Visual Communication leitest. Kannst du uns erzählen, was dich dorthin geführt hat?
Sarah Owens Ich habe in Deutschland Kommunikationsdesign studiert und dann eine Zeit lang als Editorial und Corporate Designerin gearbeitet. Ich dachte damals nicht daran, in die Designlehre zu wechseln. Dann kam die Finanzkrise nach der Dotcom-Blase – viele Menschen hatten zu viel in Online-Unternehmen investiert. Ich zog von einem Verlag zum nächsten, von einem Designstudio zum nächsten. Und dann dachte ich mir, das wäre jetzt der richtige Zeitpunkt zum Weiterstudieren, was ich schon immer machen wollte. Ich bewarb mich beim Royal College of Art / V&A (Victoria & Albert Museum) in London auf ein Studium in Designgeschichte. Dort lernte ich, wie Design betrachtet werden kann und wie es historisch betrachtet wurde. Es ging wirklich darum, Design als Ausdruck von Kultur zu verstehen. Ich las mich in die Soziologie und die Kulturtheorie ein und erweiterte so meine Vorstellung über Design. Ich wollte herausfinden, warum Designerinnen und Designer das tun, was sie tun, und warum sie so ausgebildet werden, wie sie ausgebildet werden. Der nächste Schritt war dann das Doktorat. Das war für mich offensichtlich, denn ich wollte nicht mehr in die Praxis zurück. Ein Doktorat schien mir der beste Weg, um mehr über das gestalterische Berufsfeld zu lernen. Nachdem ich einige Jahre an meiner Dissertation gearbeitet hatte, entschied ich mich für eine akademische Karriere und begann, mich auf Stellen zu bewerben. Die Designlehre erschien mir perfekt, denn in diesem Bereich konnte ich Theorie, Praxis und Geschichte vereinen. Ich konnte Design mit anderen Disziplinen verknüpfen, mit jungen Designerinnen und Designern über die Rolle des Designs sprechen und darüber, was sie ändern wollten. In diesem Umfeld konnte ich alle Interessen einbringen, die ich über die Jahre angesammelt hatte. Das tönt nach einer sehr gradlinigen Laufbahn, aber die Designlehre war für mich am Anfang kein Karriereziel. Es ist eher so, dass sich eines zum anderen fügte. Ich war immer sehr interessiert und neugierig auf gewisse Dinge.
VS Deine Arbeit in Zürich ist auf jeden Fall visionär, was unter anderem mit dieser Auszeichnung gewürdigt wird. Du siehst deine Tätigkeit an der ZHdK bestimmt vor allem auch als ein Niederreissen des Elfenbeinturms, in dem sich das akademische Design verschanzt, und als Versuch, die Studierenden zu erreichen und ihnen Design als eine Disziplin zu vermitteln, die viel einflussreicher sein kann, als es die Tradition im 20. Jahrhundert definiert hat. Du arbeitest jetzt seit zehn Jahren in Zürich. In deinem Departement hattest du verschiedene Funktionen und leitest nun den Master in Visual Communication und die Visual Research Unit, was deinem Interesse für die Designforschung entspricht. Ich möchte kurz über deine Laufbahn sprechen, die nicht linear war, sondern unterbrochen von sehr interessanten Wendepunkten. Zuerst einmal dein Stipendium an der Akademie Schloss Solitude in Stuttgart 2009, das dir auch den Raum verschafft hat für deine vielen Ideen, über die du bereits nachgedacht hattest. Kannst du uns mehr darüber erzählen?
SO 2009 hatte ich gerade ein Buch fertig geschrieben, zwei Jahre an meinem Doktorat gearbeitet und war mit vielen Dingen beschäftigt. Das Stipendium der *Akademie Schloss Solitude* war ein sehr willkommener Unterbruch. Ich musste nichts produzieren. Ich hatte Zeit, mich in Philosophie und Sozialanthropologie einzulesen, mit Leuten aus den bildenden Künsten, der Architektur, der Musik oder dem Tanz zu sprechen. Für mich war es eine Verschnaufpause in einem Kreislauf, in dem ich von einem Termin zu nächsten hetzte und versuchte, meinen Weg als Akademikerin zu finden. Plötzlich hatte ich die Freiheit, die Ideen einfach so kommen zu lassen. Ich stellte fest, dass mein Ansatz sehr disziplinär war. Ich betrachtete das Design als Designerin. So war ich ausgebildet worden. Ich hatte Designgeschichte studiert und blieb natürlich im Designdiskurs. Aber ich hatte den Eindruck, dass sich viele Disziplinen und Sparten mit Design beschäftigten und nicht unbedingt denselben Blickwinkel hatten. Deshalb organisierte ich zwei Jahre später zusammen mit Björn Franke, der ebenfalls ein Stipendiat war, ein Symposium auf Schloss Solitude. Wir wollten Design als grundlegende menschliche Aktivität erforschen und wählten einen sehr interdisziplinären Ansatz, um beispielsweise zu erforschen, wie wir uns als Menschen selbst gestalten. Wir luden Referentinnen und Referenten aus verschiedenen Bereichen ein, über Design zu sprechen. Unser Ziel war es, diese Bereiche zu verbinden, die Diskussion zu öffnen und eine breitere Perspektive einzunehmen.
VS Ich finde das sehr interessant: Die Idee, dass keine Ergebnisse nötig waren, dass der konstante Druck zum ständigen Produzieren wegfiel, den sich die Akademie und das Design selbst auferlegen. Dass du einen offenen Raum hattest, wo neue Ideen in einem interdisziplinären

L. *Making / Crafting / Designing* symposium at Akademie Schloss Solitude Stuttgart, 2011

"amateur design" – PowerPoint presentations, websites, notices, etc., that designers who are not formally trained as designers make or produce. I wanted to find out how everyday designers understand design. How do they make sense of a design task? What knowledge are their decisions based on? Again, I turned to the social sciences, to sociology and ethnography, since I did not want to look at everyday design only in terms of aesthetics, but consider it as a social practice. This was important because when I was interviewing everyday designers, I had to find new ways to speak with them about design, and also to learn from them. I could not rely on the professional discourse that I had been taught, so we did not talk about micro-typography, ligatures or similar things, because other aspects were more important to their way of designing. The research made me take a completely new perspective, since I was also used to professional designers dismissing this kind of design. That's because in formal design education, students are taught that this is what professional designers distance themselves from. On the other hand, everyday design makes up a large part of our visual culture. It surrounds us. So in the research process I had to, in a sense, unlearn my own design education. I had to find new ways of framing the process or thinking about what's important. This led me to ask "who is actually defining everyday designers as 'amateurs', people who don't know what they are doing? Who is drawing these boundaries?" With this, the scope of my research expanded to professional designers – me included – and the relationship between professional and everyday designers. I recognised that when we as professional designers define outsiders, we also define ourselves. If, for example, professional designers say that everyday designers design unconsciously or that they decide according to personal preferences, this means, in turn, that professional designers design consciously and decide according to other, more objective criteria. It was very interesting to look at how professional designers think about themselves and how this establishes a boundary. Through this, I started to retreat from a professional viewpoint, since I was trying to simply observe this relationship. The methods I used transformed me in the process. I felt I was a completely different person with a very different perspective after having done the research.

VS   So not only do we create disciplinary silos within design education, we also create very strong boundaries that define who is allowed in and who is not. And of course that creates a hierarchy and issues of value, because then your work as a professional designer is valued more, paid more than the work of an amateur or an everyday designer, as you mentioned. But it also speaks to a certain elitism, still very present in the design discipline, which is fundamentally a hindrance to its progression and natural evolution. One of the first research projects you were involved in, not so much as a lead researcher but as a co-researcher, was *Art.School.Differences* in 2014 and 2015. It also investigated the methods by which institutions exclude and include certain voices. Could you say a few words about that?

SO   It was a project that was initiated by several researchers in different art schools. As a co-researcher, I had the freedom to define a project within the overall thematic scope. I chose to look at graphic design education, and looked for a phrase or a concept that would enable me to examine mechanisms of exclusion – specifically those I have experienced in my own design education, or that often surface in general statements about design education, but also those I observe in the teaching that we do. I took a phrase that I hear quite often, which is "good design" or the "good designer". This phrase and the associated concept have normative aspects: "good" is, for instance, something that is morally good. It proposes certain ideas about what designers do, or about who can become a designer. And although it is only a single phrase, it encapsulates multiple normative narratives. This got me into thinking more about narratives or myths in design education that shape or normalise certain attitudes, values or beliefs that all of us – students, educators and practitioners – might have about design. And these assumptions and ideas bring with them certain protocols that influence how we select students, how we define excellence, or who gets to graduate. These narratives can also be very much disconnected from the actual situations of students. For instance, if the "good designer" is a person who works all day and night, then all of those students who have family responsibilities, or who have other responsibilities that might impact on their practice, cannot become "good designers". Here, again, was the question about who draws the boundaries, who creates these definitions? What was remarkable about that project was that we were encouraged not to remain at the level of analysis, but also to look for situations or possibilities of change, for instance in the admissions process, in order to counteract mechanisms we observed.

VS   Did the outcomes of that research have an impact on how you consider admissions: who gets in and who doesn't? I can imagine it changed things in your practice, but did it also change things in institutions where you operate?

SO   Good question. These kinds of changes are very small. They are not changes that can be boldly proclaimed. I do

M.   MA Visual Communication workshop at Zurich University of the Arts, 2019 © Björn Franke

N. Installation for the research project *Art.School.Differences*, 2016 © Sarah Owens

Kontext entstehen konnten. Kannst du uns erzählen, wie dieses Verständnis und der Bezug zu den Sozialwissenschaften, den du erwähnt hast, in der Forschung für deine Dissertation zusammenkommen?

SO   Klar. Ich doktorierte an der Universität Reading und erforschte ein Thema, das sich aus meiner Masterarbeit ergab. Ich interessierte mich für die «Amateurgrafik», wie es die professionellen Designerinnen und Designer nennen würden: PowerPoint-Präsentationen, Websites oder Aushänge, die von Leuten gestaltet werden, die keine formale Designausbildung durchlaufen haben. Ich wollte wissen, wie Alltagsdesignerinnen und -designer das Gestalten verstehen. Wie gehen sie an eine Designaufgabe heran? Auf welchem Wissen basieren ihre Entscheidungen? Ich bewegte mich einmal mehr in den Sozialwissenschaften, in Soziologie und Ethnografie, denn ich wollte das Alltagsdesign nicht nur in Bezug auf die Ästhetik betrachten, sondern als soziale Praxis. Das war wichtig, denn als ich Alltagsdesignerinnen und -designer interviewte, musste ich mit ihnen auf eine andere Art und Weise über Design sprechen und versuchen, von ihnen zu lernen. Ich konnte mich nicht an den professionellen Diskurs halten, den ich gelernt hatte. Wir sprachen also nicht über Mikro-Typografie, Ligaturen oder Ähnliches, denn in ihrer Gestaltung waren andere Aspekte wichtiger. Die Forschung verlieh mir eine völlig neue Perspektive, denn sonst war ich es gewohnt, dass professionelle Designerinnen und Designer Alltagsdesign ablehnten. Das kommt daher, dass die Studierenden in der formalen Designausbildung lernen, dass sie sich von dieser Art des Gestaltens abheben müssen. Das Alltagsdesign macht aber einen grossen Teil unserer visuellen Kultur aus. Es umgibt uns. Während der Forschungsarbeit musste ich meine eigene Designausbildung also sozusagen entlernen. Ich musste neue Wege finden, um Prozesse einzuordnen und abzuschätzen, was wichtig ist. Ich fragte mich deshalb: Wer definiert eigentlich Alltagsdesignerinnen und -designer als «Amateure»? Wer definiert sie als Leute, die angeblich keine Ahnung von Gestaltung haben? Wer zieht diese Grenzen? Damit weitete sich der Fokus meiner Forschungen aus, auf professionelle Designerinnen und Designer – mich eingeschlossen – und auf die Beziehungen zwischen Profis und Alltagsdesignerinnen und -designern. Ich erkannte, dass wir professionelle Designerinnen und Designer auch uns selbst definieren, wenn wir festlegen, wer die Aussenstehenden sind. Wenn professionelle Designerinnen und Designer zum Beispiel sagen, dass die Alltagsdesignerinnen und -designer unbewusst gestalten oder anhand persönlicher Vorlieben entscheiden, bedeutet das umgekehrt auch, dass professionelle bewusst gestalten und anhand objektiver Kriterien entscheiden. Es war sehr interessant zu untersuchen, wie professionelle Designerinnen und Designer über sich selbst denken und wie dadurch eine Grenze gezogen wird. Ich zog mich deshalb von einem professionelle Standpunkt zurück, denn ich wollte ganz einfach diese Beziehung beobachten. Die Methoden meiner Forschung haben mich mit der Zeit verändert. Ich fühlte mich danach als eine ganz andere Person mit einer ganz anderen Perspektive.

VS   Wir erschaffen in der Designlehre also nicht nur disziplinäre Kategorien, sondern auch klare Grenzen, die bestimmen, wer dazugehört und wer nicht. Daraus entstehen natürlich Hierarchien und Wertevorstellungen, weil dann das professionelle Schaffen mehr wert ist und besser bezahlt wird als Amateur- oder Alltagsdesign, wie du sagtest. Es geht auch um ein elitäres Denken, das im Design noch immer sehr präsent ist und es vor allem daran hindert, Fortschritte zu machen und sich natürlich zu entwickeln. *Art.School.Differences* war 2014 und 2015 eines der ersten Forschungsprojekte, an dem du beteiligt warst. Es untersuchte auch die Methoden, mit denen Institutionen gewisse Stimmen ein- oder ausschliessen. Kannst du uns ein bisschen mehr darüber sagen?

SO   Das Projekt wurde von mehreren Forschenden aus verschiedenen Kunstschulen initiiert. Also hatte ich die Freiheit, ein Projekt innerhalb des allgemeinen Themenrahmens zu erarbeiten. Ich betrachtete die Grafikdesign-Ausbildung und suchte nach Formulierungen oder einem Begriff, der es erlauben würde, Ausschlussmechanismen zu untersuchen – vor allem diejenigen, die ich in meiner eigenen Designausbildung erfahren hatte oder die in allgemeinen Aussagen über die Designausbildung erscheinen, aber auch diejenigen, die ich in unserem Unterricht beobachte. Eine Formulierung hörte ich besonders oft: «gute Gestaltung» und davon abgeleitet «gute Gestalter». Die Formulierung und die Idee dahinter sind normativ: «Gut» ist zum Beispiel auch, was moralisch «gut» ist. Es bringt gewisse Vorstellungen darüber hervor, was Designerinnen und Designer tun und wer Designerin oder Designer werden kann. Es ist nur eine einzelne Formulierung, aber sie schliesst viele normative Erzählungen ein. Das brachte mich dazu, über Narrative oder Mythen in der Designausbildung nachzudenken, die gewisse Haltungen, Werte oder Ideen formen oder normalisieren, die wir alle – Studierende, Lehrende, Praktizierende – über Design haben können. Diese

think they become visible in that we have a more diverse student body, or that we allow for more flexibility within the curriculum, or that the conversations that we have across institutions go in a direction where topics of who is inside and who is outside increasingly come to the fore. Our idea of the typical graphic designer is a very homogenous picture of a certain type of person. Maybe we can change this picture, based on wanting to go in a different direction, to include more perspectives and more diverse experiences. In this sense, the changes are not measurable. But there is an atmosphere or attitude that I think signals that things are going in a different and better direction.

VS	Another side of your career that has been developing steadily over recent years is activism, as something that has to happen in parallel to your work as a design educator. You are active within academia and design education, fields that can be seen as ivory towers, inaccessible to many, and you've been working on a variety of fronts to get out of them. One example is the *Black Film Festival Zurich*, which you started and continue to be involved in. Could you tell us about how you've been trying to connect to the communities around you in different ways?

SO	The *Black Film Festival Zurich* debuted in 2019, and was co-organised by Rispa Stephen and Ania Mathis. The basic idea was to show feature-length films and short films that are either by black filmmakers or show some aspect of black experiences. We also have certain aims: we want to show films that are from around the world, not just the US context, and not only the African continent, but from the African diaspora worldwide. Also, it is very important to us to highlight non-stereotypical narratives and forms of representation. Both of these are activist aims. On the other hand, it is a film festival, so we want the films to be enjoyable and do not want to seem overly didactic in the sense of "we need to talk about these narratives." Of course there is a significant difference for me between teaching a film seminar about black film and actually co-creating a festival for which we can pick films that are not shown anywhere else and make them available to the community. One of the starting points for us was also that a lot of the films that are hailed as fundamental for black cinema in film history nevertheless had stereotypical ideas behind them. The black protagonists are poor or uneducated. They need a white saviour to get them out of poverty. We didn't see enough films that show other types of protagonists or stories. We wanted to see black protagonists who are not caricatures, but complex figures. So on the one hand, our selection and showing of films is a comment on the film industry, saying that there is not enough diversity, not just concerning filmmakers, producers and actors, but also in the types of stories that are told. And on the other hand, it is a comment on representation and identity. At the same time, they're films you can simply watch and enjoy. So there are several levels of access. For me, to be able to leave the ivory tower, as you said, is also crucial. This is because the conversations outside of the academic environment are just different kinds of conversations and very enriching. Bringing a community together in viewing the films and talking about them is what I enjoy so much about this kind of work.

VS	With the activist side of your practice, you create spaces that previously were not there but you also create spaces for conversations that didn't exist previously. That again parallels your work within the educational institution. For me, what is very interesting is this idea of making and claiming space and also of imagining otherwise, because as you said, if you don't see certain people in certain roles all around you, why would you think that a person like you can be in those roles? So the lack of role models and the lack of representation is endemic not only in our everyday life, but very pointedly in design education itself. What are your priorities right now?

SO	The interests that I have at the moment are ones I've carried with me for a while and I try to reconfigure them in different ways, to see how some questions suddenly connect to others, although maybe two years ago, they seemed very far apart. These questions keep revolving around issues of representation, visibility, knowledge, language, and also politics. For instance, I am interested in how certain visual representations produce otherness within our current media. I am interested in the unknown and the unseen, in things that are hidden and might want to remain hidden, where visibility might not be desirable. At the same time, non-visibility may somehow link to a hypervisibility. These are very general questions that I have. They don't necessarily need to lead to a research paper or a certain outcome. It's more that they keep emerging in the teaching that I do; they pop up in research projects that I'm involved in. But what unites some of these questions is again the process of unlearning, of bracketing knowledge and really opening up to other views. I know that when we acquire knowledge, it tends to appear very precious, as in: "I worked so hard to know this and to understand this, it's difficult to let it go." But I see unlearning not as a process of losing something: it's more an interrogation of what you've learnt and why you have learnt it. It allows you to learn something about your learning. And this helps with developing a different or new perspective on an issue. If I can understand what my

0.   Research project *Swiss Graphic Design and Typography Revisited*, 2016–20

P. *Black Film Festival Zurich*, 2021 © Ann Kern

Annahmen und Ideen bringen auch gewisse Verfahren mit sich, die einen Einfluss darauf haben, wie wir Studierende auswählen, wie wir Exzellenz definieren und wer einen Abschluss erhält. Diese Narrative sind manchmal auch sehr weit von den tatsächlichen Situationen der Studierenden entfernt. Wenn «gute Designerinnen und Designer» beispielsweise diejenigen Personen sind, die Tag und Nacht arbeiten, heisst das, dass all jene Studierenden, deren Arbeitszeit auch von familiären oder anderen Verpflichtungen beansprucht wird, keine «guten Designerinnen und Designer» werden können. Auch hier stellt sich die Frage, wer diese Grenzen zieht, wer die Definitionen aufstellt. Bemerkenswert an diesem Projekt war, dass wir Forschenden ermutigt wurden, nicht auf der Analyseebene zu bleiben, sondern auch nach Möglichkeiten zur Veränderung zu suchen, zum Beispiel im Aufnahmeprozess, um den beobachteten Mechanismen etwas entgegenzusetzen.

VS Haben die Ergebnisse dieser Forschung einen Einfluss darauf, wie du das Aufnahmeverfahren betrachtest, und darauf, wer aufgenommen wird und wer nicht? Ich kann mir vorstellen, dass sie deine Arbeit verändert haben, aber haben sie auch die Institutionen verändert, in denen du dich bewegst?

SO Das ist eine gute Frage. Es sind sehr kleine und subtile Änderungen, keine grossen Gesten. Ich denke, sie werden dadurch sichtbar, dass wir mehr Diversität unter den Studierenden haben, dass wir mehr Flexibilität im Curriculum zulassen oder dass bei Gesprächen mit anderen Institutionen die Themen von Dazugehörigkeit und Ausschluss eher in den Vordergrund treten. Unsere Idee von typischen Grafikdesignerinnen und -designern ist ein sehr homogenes Bild eines gewissen Personentyps. Vielleicht können wir dieses Bild ändern, wenn wir uns in eine andere Richtung bewegen und mehr Perspektiven und vielfältigere Erfahrungen einbeziehen. In diesem Sinne lassen sich die Veränderungen nicht messen. Aber ich denke, die momentane Stimmung oder Haltung zeigt an, dass sich die Dinge zum Besseren ändern.

VS Ein anderer Teil deiner Karriere, den du in den letzten Jahren entwickelt hast, ist das gesellschaftliche Engagement, das du parallel zu deiner Arbeit als Designdozentin einbringst. Du bist in der Hochschule und der Designlehre aktiv, in Bereichen also, die als Elfenbeintürme gelten und für viele unzugänglich sind. Gleichzeitig setzt du dich an verschiedenen Orten dafür ein, diese zu durchbrechen. Ein Beispiel ist das *Black Film Festival Zurich*, das du mitgegründet hast und an dem du noch immer beteiligt bist. Kannst du uns erzählen, wie du versuchst, den Kontakt zu den Gemeinschaften aufzubauen, die dich umgeben?

SO Das *Black Film Festival Zurich* wurde 2019 gegründet und von Rispa Stephen, Ania Mathis und mir gemeinsam organisiert. Die Grundidee war, abendfüllende Spielfilme und Kurzfilme zu zeigen, die entweder von schwarzen Filmemacherinnen und Filmemachern gedreht wurden oder die sich mit Erfahrungen von schwarzen Menschen befassen. Wir haben bestimmte Ziele: Wir wollen Filme aus der ganzen Welt zeigen, nicht nur aus dem US-Kontext und auch nicht nur aus afrikanischen Ländern, sondern aus der afrikanischen Diaspora weltweit. Es ist uns sehr wichtig, nichtstereotype Narrative und Darstellungsformen hervorzuheben. Das sind aktivistische Ziele. Andererseits ist es ein Filmfestival und wir wollen, dass die Filme auch unterhaltsam sind. Wir wollen nicht überdidaktisch sein im Sinne von: «Wir müssen jetzt über diese Narrative sprechen». Für mich gibt es natürlich einen grossen Unterschied zwischen einem Filmseminar über schwarzen Filme und der Mitorganisation eines Festivals, für das wir Filme auswählen können, die sonst nirgendwo gezeigt werden, um sie so der Öffentlichkeit zugänglich zu machen. Ein Ausgangspunkt für uns war, dass viele der Filme, die in der Filmgeschichte als bedeutend für das schwarze Kino gelten, eigentlich auf stereotypen Ideen begründet sind. Deren schwarze Protagonistinnen und Protagonisten sind arm und schlecht ausgebildet. Sie müssen von weissen Menschen aus ihrer Armut gerettet werden. Wir fanden nicht genug Filme, die andere Figuren oder Geschichten zeigten. Wir wollten schwarze Protagonistinnen und Protagonisten sehen, die keine Karikaturen, sondern komplexe Figuren sind. Unser Filmprogramm ist daher einerseits ein Kommentar über die Filmindustrie und besagt, dass diese nicht genügend Diversität aufweist. Das betrifft nicht nur Filmemacherinnen und Filmemacher, Produzentinnen und Produzenten oder Schauspielerinnen und Schauspieler, sondern auch die Arten von Geschichten, die erzählt werden. Andererseits ist es auch ein Kommentar über Repräsentation und Identität. Und gleichzeitig sind es Filme, die wir auch einfach schauen und geniessen können. Es gibt also verschiedene Zugangsebenen. Wie du sagtest, ist es für mich auch sehr wichtig, ab und zu den Elfenbeinturm zu verlassen. Gespräche ausserhalb des akademischen

perspective is based on, then I can more readily try to take a different position or perspective. I have been trying to explore this with our graduate students. They already come with design skills and practical experience, and we encourage them to develop a new perspective on what they do or an issue that is very important to them. In our conversations, their questions and interests interconnect with my questions or the things that I am personally interested in. For example, we recently did a seminar on images and affect. We read poetry, we looked at paintings, we looked at performances. We also talked about how images affect us personally. These are the kinds of conversations that are inspiring for me, and I hope they are for the students as well, to help them identify what is important to them, or which new direction they want to go in, or what kind of approach or practice they want to establish when they graduate.

VS   The world is changing at an alarming speed. We're not just talking about right now, with the climate crisis and the current pandemic. As you said, we need to revise and question how we educate our designers. Because if you continue educating them under the 20th-century paradigm, using a model originally crystallised by the Bauhaus experiments, and the sort of linear narrative that came out of retelling that history over the next 50 or 60 years, it certainly seems very different from the world today. Shouldn't we adapt the way we educate to match the world around us? You could think of a crisis as a great opportunity as, say, neo-liberal capitalist thinking postulates, but also as an opportunity in a less formal way: a space or pause, a limbo that is created for some significant change to happen. I would argue that design education is at a moment of deep uncertainty, not just in Switzerland, but everywhere, especially in Western Europe and North America, because those are the regions that have implemented this modern idea of design and design education on a greater scale and that replicated it in turn. It has also spread to other places in the world because the Bauhaus model is so prevalent, but it seems to me that in those regions at least, people proudly hold on to this. Wouldn't it be a great advantage for all of us to fundamentally question it, to position ourselves in relation to it and then think it through together to come up with something else?

SO   I completely agree. The old formulas do not work because the problems we are dealing with currently are highly complex. Or maybe the problems we encounter have always been complex, but we have not realised this until now. We used to think that a poster could "solve" poverty and now we are seeing that actually, some people may have noticed the poster we designed, but even this awareness cannot provide a solution to a highly complex problem that involves many stakeholders with very different interests. This pandemic forces us to rethink and also to interrogate what we have been doing so far. We're forced to rethink our relations, our values and what we hope for. We also must rethink what we consider as truth or what we really believe in, so that in that sense, it is good that we cannot just continue in our routine ways. This applies also to the way that design is taught, or more generally to the idea that there is a universal way to design, that if students learn to handle shapes and colours and fonts, they will do great design. We can leave these formulas behind us because we know they do not work. There are other notions and positions we need to add and the students are reminding us of this. In these times of uncertainty, we are noticing how difficult it is to deal with not knowing what is going to happen after the crisis ends, where we are going to end up or how design is going to change. For the students personally, the question also is whether they are going to have a job. That means that design educators have to react. What we can do, or what I try to do, is turn this into a topic and say: "Let's try to deal with the unknown. Let's try to learn to bear the deep insecurity that this brings with it." If we take a more research-oriented, inquiring approach, we might not see the exact final outcome in front of us during the design process, but at least we can see the next step. For this, we must remain open to diversions and to unexpected things that might lead us somewhere else. When students approach design in a way that is not universalist or overly prescriptive, where they have the opportunity to fully attend to the actual phenomenon, and the possibility to say, "I don't know what's going to come out of this" or "at least I found out that this doesn't work", it will hopefully equip them to deal with uncertainty without becoming completely unable to do anything. The risk is that they feel so disconcerted and hopeless that they think this is not worth anything anymore. Of course we don't – I don't – want that to happen.

VS   You were also saying that if we continue to teach design with the idea of problem-solving, solution-oriented practice we're not going to get out of that, and students will feel paralysed because they cannot come up with a solution. But if we expand our understanding of what we need to do into one much more related to listening, mediating, figuring out, can we actually bring something into this conversation? This ties back to what we were talking about: how you yourself learned how to listen, to have different kinds of conversations, and that is informed by your work with the communities around you, outside of academia, your knowledge of the social sciences and their tools, and also

Q.   Roxane Gay and Sarah Owens at *Literatur Festival Zurich*, 2019 © Johanna Saxen

Umfelds sind einfach anders und sehr bereichernd. Was ich an dieser Arbeit so schätze, ist, dass durch das Sehen der Filme und das gemeinsame Diskutieren eine Gemeinschaft entsteht.

vs Mit der aktivistischen Seite deiner Tätigkeit schaffst du Räume, die es zuvor nicht gab, Räume für Gespräche, die zuvor nicht geführt wurden. Das ist wiederum eine Parallele zu deiner Arbeit an der Hochschule. Ich finde besonders die Idee interessant, Räume zu schaffen und einzufordern und auch andere Vorstellungen zu entwickeln, denn – wie du sagst – wenn bestimmte Menschen nicht bestimmte Rollen einnehmen können, wie soll man dann davon ausgehen, dass man selbst eine solche Rolle einnehmen kann? Der Mangel an Rollenvorbildern und Repräsentation ist nicht nur im Alltag allgegenwärtig, sondern vor allem auch in der Designlehre. Wo liegen im Moment deine Prioritäten?

so Meine aktuellen Interessen trage ich schon eine Zeit lang mit mir herum. Ich versuche, sie auf verschiedene Arten zusammenzusetzen, um zu erkennen, wie bestimmte Fragen plötzlich mit anderen verknüpft werden können, auch wenn sie zwei Jahre zuvor vielleicht noch weit voneinander entfernt schienen. Diese Fragen drehen sich um Themen von Darstellung, Sichtbarkeit, Wissen, Sprache oder auch Politik. Ich interessiere mich zum Beispiel dafür, wie bestimmte visuelle Darstellungen in den gängigen Medien Otherness erzeugen. Mich interessiert das Unbekannte und Ungesehene, die versteckten Dinge, die vielleicht versteckt bleiben wollen und keine Sichtbarkeit wünschen. Gleichzeitig kann Nicht-Visibilität auch mit Hypervisibilität einhergehen. Das sind ganz allgemeine Fragen, die ich mir stelle. Daraus muss nicht unbedingt ein Artikel oder ein bestimmtes Ergebnis entstehen. Eher kommen sie immer wieder in meinem Unterricht vor und tauchen in Forschungsprojekten auf, an denen ich beteiligt bin. Was einige dieser Fragen verbindet, ist erneut der Prozess des Entlernens, die Fähigkeit, vorhandenes Wissen auszuklammern und sich wirklich für andere Ansichten zu öffnen. Ich weiss, dass bereits erworbenes Wissen als etwas sehr Wertvolles angesehen wird, im Sinne von: «Ich habe hart gearbeitet, um das zu wissen und zu verstehen, und es ist schwierig, loszulassen.» Aber ich sehe das Entlernen nicht als einen Verlust. Es ist ein Hinterfragen des Gelernten und der Gründe für das Erlernen. Dadurch lernen wir etwas über unser Lernen. Und das hilft uns, einen anderen, neuen Blickwinkel zu finden. Wenn ich verstehe, worauf meine Perspektive aufbaut, kann ich leichter eine andere Position oder Perspektive einnehmen. Ich versuche, das mit meinen Master-Studierenden zu erforschen. Sie verfügen bereits über umfassende Designkenntnisse und praktische Erfahrung und wir fördern sie darin, eine neue Perspektive auf ihre Tätigkeit oder ein für sie wichtiges Thema zu entwickeln. In unseren Gesprächen verbinden sich ihre Fragen und Interessen mit meinen. Kürzlich haben wir zum Beispiel ein Seminar über Bilder und Affekttheorie veranstaltet. Wir lasen Gedichte, betrachteten Gemälde und Performances. Wir sprachen auch darüber, wie uns Bilder persönlich beeinflussen. Solche Gespräche inspirieren mich sehr und ich hoffe, dass das auch für die Studierenden gilt, dass sie ihnen zu erkennen helfen, was für sie wichtig ist, welche neue Richtung sie einschlagen wollen oder welchen Ansatz und welche Praxis sie nach ihrem Studium aufbauen wollen.

vs Die Welt verändert sich besorgniserregend schnell. Und zwar nicht nur gerade jetzt mit der Klimakrise und der Pandemie. Wie du sagtest, müssen wir überdenken und hinterfragen, wie wir unsere Designerinnen und Designer ausbilden. Wenn wir sie weiterhin nach dem Paradigma des 20. Jahrhunderts ausbilden und dabei ein Modell anwenden, das aus den Bauhaus-Experimenten entstanden war, und weiterhin das gradlinige Narrativ pflegen, das sich während 50 oder 60 Jahren daraus ergeben hat, dann ist das meilenweit von der heutigen Welt entfernt. Sollten wir unsere Ausbildungen nicht der Welt um uns herum anpassen? Eine Krise kann als wichtige Chance verstanden werden, wie es etwa das neoliberale kapitalistische Denken fordert, aber auch als eine Gelegenheit in einem weniger strengen Sinn: als Raum oder Pause, als Vakuum, das dazu da ist, eine bedeutende Veränderung zu ermöglichen. Ich denke, die Designlehre befindet sich in einer Zeit der grossen Unsicherheit, dies nicht nur in der Schweiz, sondern weltweit und vor allem in Westeuropa und Nordamerika. Das sind die Regionen, die diese moderne Idee des Designs und der Designlehre grossflächig eingeführt und reproduziert haben. Das vorherrschende Bauhaus-Modell verbreitete sich zwar auch an anderen Orten auf der Welt, aber es scheint mir, als würden diese Regionen starr daran festhalten. Wäre es nicht für uns alle ein grosser Vorteil, es grundlegend zu hinterfragen, unsere eigene Position dazu einzunehmen, es zusammen zu überdenken, um dann etwas anderes einzubringen?

so Das sehe ich genauso. Die alten Formeln funktionieren nicht, weil die Probleme, mit denen wir zu tun haben, äusserst komplex sind. Oder vielleicht waren unsere Probleme schon immer komplex, aber wir haben es bis jetzt nicht bemerkt. Wir dachten zum Beispiel, ein Plakat könnte das Problem der Armut «lösen», und jetzt merken wir, dass auch wenn einige Leute unser Plakat tatsächlich wahrnehmen, diese Aufmerksamkeit keine Lösung für ein höchst komplexes Problem wie das der Armut bietet, das viele Beteiligte mit ganz unterschiedlichen Interessen involviert. Die Pandemie zwingt uns dazu, Dinge zu überdenken und das zu hinterfragen, was wir bisher getan hatten. Wir sind dazu gezwungen, unsere Beziehungen zu überdenken, und wir sind dazu gezwungen, unsere Werte und Hoffnungen zu überdenken. Wir müssen überdenken, was wir als Wahrheit betrachten und woran wir glauben. In diesem Sinn ist es gut, dass wir nicht einfach mit unseren Routinen weitermachen können. Das gilt auch für die Art und Weise, wie Design unterrichtet wird, und allgemeiner für die Idee, dass es angeblich eine universell gültige Art des Gestaltens gibt. Dass beispielsweise Studierende nur lernen müssen, mit Formen, Farben und Schriften umzugehen, um grossartiges Design zu erzielen. Wir können solche Formeln hinter uns lassen, weil wir wissen, dass sie nicht funktionieren. Es gibt andere Begriffe und Positionen, die wir hinzufügen müssen – die Studierenden erinnern uns daran. In diesen unsicheren Zeiten wird uns bewusst, wie schwierig es ist, damit umzugehen, dass wir nicht wissen, was nach der Krise passieren wird, wo wir landen oder wie sich das Design verändert. Für die Studentinnen und Studenten persönlich geht es auch darum, ob sie Arbeit haben werden. Das heisst, wir Lehrenden müssen reagieren. Was wir tun können, oder was ich zumindest versuche, ist dieses Thema zur Sprache zu bringen: «Versuchen wir mit dem Unbekannten umzugehen. Versuchen wir zu lernen, die grosse Unsicherheit auszuhalten, die die Situation mit sich bringt.» Mit einem stärker forschungsorientierten, experimentellen Ansatz sehen wir während dem Designprozess vielleicht nicht genau, was am Ende dabei herauskommt, aber wir sehen zumindest den nächsten Schritt. Dazu müssen wir gegenüber Umwegen und Unerwartetem offen bleiben,

R. Research project *Wolfgang Weingart: Typography in Context* leading to an exhibition at Museum für Gestaltung Zürich, 2014 © Betty Fleck

this general curiosity about interdisciplinarity and just sharing and finding overlaps and interesting potentials for collaboration. Maybe that could be a way out. What do you think of that sort of paradigm change; and, perhaps as a concluding thought, which ideas could we hold onto in order to believe that we can make it happen?

SO To approach the design process in new ways, maybe more exploratively, or in an even more open-ended way at least gives the possibility to say: "Let's rethink this whole thing. Let's rethink criteria that we have. Let's have this paradigm change." But we need to be aware of what we want, of course. I don't see this process as destroying or losing something. It's really more a reimagining and rebuilding. I have the feeling that avoiding universalism and being more aware of the complexity and multi-layeredness of experiences is already a good starting point. I think it's a good starting point also for seeing how we construct, navigate and make sense of the world based on the very different conditions we find ourselves in or were born into. Also, I think it is very important to remain attentive to our blind spots so that we don't simply want everything to be new, but ask ourselves what we are missing at the moment and where are we biased. It's a risky undertaking, almost an upheaval. And it cannot be done superficially. But there are more and more people who are ready to try something else in order to address these problems otherwise. We as designers make ourselves irrelevant if we merely talk about form and colour, and cannot connect to other conversations or express what we can bring to these problems and issues, for instance by making them experienceable or by adopting new perspectives. I've been trying to find new words to describe this total investment in an issue, because I find that many students nowadays are willing to dive into something completely, to almost be overwhelmed by something. That needs a certain level of trust, of compassion, and a willingness to develop one's ability to listen and to observe, and to change oneself. If we have design students who want to approach the world differently, then we will have future designers who will change design practice. Maybe we won't be focused so much on products, but more on asking questions, and from this, a new discourse will result. I think what I'm trying to do is make the boundaries of design more porous. I don't want to be hermetically sealed off from others. I want there to be a flow and I want things to adapt and not be so rigid. I guess that's what I'm working towards.

VS I think that's not only an ambitious but also a very laudable goal; I wish more practitioners were doing the same as you, Sarah. It's been a great pleasure to talk to you today. I want to thank you for your time, your openness, and the wonderful ideas you've shared. I hope that everybody who listens to this conversation comes out of it as strengthened and inspired as I am. So, thank you.

Vera Sacchetti
Design critic and curator, member
of the Swiss Federal Design Commission

da sie uns woanders hinführen können. Wenn Studierende nicht universalistisch oder normativ an das Gestalten herangehen, wenn sie die Gelegenheit haben, voll und ganz auf das eigentliche Phänomen einzugehen und sich zu sagen: «Ich weiss nicht, was daraus wird» oder «wenigstens habe ich herausgefunden, dass es nicht funktioniert», dann können sie hoffentlich mit Unsicherheit umgehen, ohne davon völlig blockiert zu werden. Es besteht sonst nämlich das Risiko, dass sie so beunruhigt und hoffnungslos sind, dass sie keinen Sinn mehr in ihrer Tätigkeit sehen. Und das wollen wir nicht – das will ich nicht.

VS Du sagst auch, dass die Idee der problemlösenden, lösungsorientierten Praxis in der Designlehre dazu führen kann, dass die Studierenden sich wie gelähmt fühlen. Denn sie können nicht immer eine Lösung finden. Wenn wir aber unser Verständnis davon, was wir brauchen, ausweiten und uns mehr auf das Zuhören, Vermitteln und Herausfinden ausrichten – können wir dann etwas zur Diskussion beitragen? Damit kommen wir zu unserem Gespräch zurück: Du hast selbst gelernt, zuzuhören, verschiedene Arten von Gesprächen zu führen. Und das ergab sich aus deiner Arbeit mit den Gemeinschaften, die dich umgeben, ausserhalb der Akademie, aus deinen Kenntnissen der Sozialwissenschaften und ihrer Ansätze und aus deinem allgemeinen Interesse für die Interdisziplinarität und das Finden von Schnittstellen mit Potenzial für Zusammenarbeiten. Das könnte ein Ausweg sein. Was denkst du über diesen Paradigmenwechsel? Und – vielleicht als Schlussgedanke – an welchen Ideen sollten wir uns festhalten, damit wir ihn umsetzen können?

SO Das Design neu anzugehen, vielleicht mit einem offeneren, explorativen Ansatz, lässt uns zumindest sagen: «Überdenken wir das Ganze, überdenken wir unsere Kriterien, ändern wir die Paradigmen». Aber wir müssen uns bewusst sein, was wir wollen. Ich sehe diesen Prozess nicht als Zerstörung oder Verlust. Es ist mehr ein Neudenken und Umbauen. Ich denke, wenn wir den Universalismus vermeiden und uns der Komplexität und Vielschichtigkeit der Erfahrungen stärker bewusst sind, ist das schon ein guter Anfang. Auch um zu verstehen, wie wir die Welt konstruieren, begreifen, uns in ihr bewegen anhand der ganz unterschiedlichen Bedingungen, in denen wir uns befinden oder in die wir hineingeboren werden. Ich denke auch, wir müssen auf unsere Schwachstellen achten, damit wir nicht einfach nur alles neu machen wollen, sondern uns selbst fragen, was uns im Moment fehlt und wo wir voreingenommen sind. Es ist ein riskantes Unterfangen, schon fast ein Umbruch. Und das kann nicht nur oberflächlich stattfinden. Aber es gibt immer mehr Leute, die bereit sind, etwas anderes auszuprobieren, die Probleme anders anzugehen. Als Designerinnen und Designer machen wir uns unbedeutend, wenn wir nur über Formen und Farben sprechen und uns nicht an breiteren Diskussionen beteiligen oder ausdrücken, was wir zur Verhandlung eines Problems oder eines Themas beitragen können, indem wir sie erfahrbar machen oder neue Perspektiven einnehmen. Ich versuche, neue Worte zu finden, um dieses umfassende Beteiligtsein an einer Thematik zu beschreiben, denn es scheint mir, dass heute viele Studierende eher gewillt sind, voll und ganz in etwas einzutauchen und davon fast schon überwältigt zu werden. Und das bedingt ein gewisses Vertrauen, ein gewisses Mitgefühl. Und den Willen, zuhören und beobachten zu lernen, sowie den Willen, sich selbst zu verändern. Wenn wir Designstudierende haben, die die Welt anders angehen wollen, haben wir zukünftige Designerinnen und Designer, die die Designpraxis verändern werden. Wir werden vielleicht nicht mehr so sehr auf Produkte fokussiert sein, sondern eher auf Fragen, aus denen dann ein neuer Diskurs entsteht. Ich versuche, die Grenzen des Designs durchlässiger zu machen. Ich will nicht hermetisch von anderen abgegrenzt sein. Ich will, dass es fliesst und dass die Dinge sich anpassen können und nicht so starr sind. Ich glaube, darauf arbeite ich hin.

VS Ich denke, das ist nicht nur ein ehrgeiziges, sondern auch ein sehr lobenswertes Ziel. Ich wünschte mir, mehr Dozierende würde es so machen wie du, Sarah. Es war mir ein grosses Vergnügen, heute mit dir zu sprechen. Ich danke dir für deine Zeit, deine Offenheit und die wunderbaren Ideen, die du mit uns teilst. Ich hoffe, dass alle, die unser Gespräch verfolgen, davon so gestärkt und inspiriert werden wie ich. Vielen Dank!

Vera Sacchetti
Designkritikerin und Kuratorin,
Mitglied der Eidgenössischen Designkommission